Making Sense

Also by John Habgood and published by SPCK:

Confessions of a Conservative Liberal (1988)

Making Sense

John Habgood
Archbishop of York

First published in Great Britain 1993
Society for Promoting Christian Knowledge
Holy Trinity Church
Marylebone Road
London NW1 4DU

© John Habgood 1993

British Library Cataloguing-in-Publication Data
A catalogue record for this book is available from the
British Library

ISBN 0-281-04711-1

Printed in Great Britain by
The Longdunn Press Ltd, Bristol

Contents

Foreword   1

Part One: Making Sense

1. Making Sense   5
2. Making Sense of Faith   14
3. Making Sense of Prayer   24
4. Making Moral Sense   36

Interlude:

Expanding Belief   43

Part Two: Science, Faith and Ethics

5. The Bible and Scientific Discovery   49
6. Response to Richard Dawkins   58
7. The Human Fertilization and Embryology Bill   64
8. The Perils of Trying to Know Too Much   74

Interlude:

Cruelty to Animals   87

Do Pigs Have Wings?   90

Part Three: Rights and Responsibilities

9. Human Nature and Human Rights   95
10. Finding a Moral Heart for Europe   110

Contents

11. The Role of the Churches in the International Order 123

12. Church and State 137

Interlude:

The Gulf War 150

Part Four: The Church of England

13. Catholicity 155

14. Believing and Belonging 168

15. Marketing the Church of England 171

Interlude:

Ruth 184

The Decade of Evangelism 187

Eton's 550th Anniversary 190

Part Five: On Being Liberal

16. Reflections on the Liberal Position 197

17. Rationality and Truth 208

18. Surprised by Hell 212

19. Living With Other Faiths 216

Epilogue 220

Foreword

An archbishop's work is by its very nature fragmented. He receives endless invitations to address a wide variety of groups, many of which indicate the topic on which they wish to hear him. In 1992 I prepared some forty addresses of this kind, not including sermons, most of them specially written for the occasion.

Under these conditions systematic writing becomes impossible. Nevertheless, there is, I believe, a consistency of thought underlying the varied range of material in this book. If an archbishop cannot do much creative thinking, he can at least be an interpreter. Indeed he shares the role of the clergy as a whole in attempting to be one of the official interpreters of Christian faith in the many different situations in which he finds himself. By collecting some of these attempts together it becomes possible to judge whether the interpretation is a coherent one, whether in fact it makes sense.

I normally lecture and preach from notes, rather than from a full text. The pieces published here, therefore, have been chosen largely because they were either written out in full beforehand, or subsequently reconstructed from transcripts. They do nevertheless represent the range of topics on which I usually find myself speaking. Many were delivered to secular audiences and thus do not make the kind of appeal to Christian authorities which might have been appropriate in a clearly Christian context.

An exception to this is the first group of four lectures from which the book takes its title. These are an expanded version of lectures originally given at York Minster. The other lectures, articles and sermons have been grouped according to topics. A few have appeared in print elsewhere, and I am grateful for the permissions given to reproduce them as part of this collection. All the material was written within the last five years. The Epilogue, which reviews my ten years as

Archbishop of York, has been specially written for this book.

My thanks are due to those who by their invitations have stimulated me to write; to my Lay Assistant, Raymond Barker, who has helped me in putting this collection together; to my secretaries, especially Anne Broadbent, who has done most of the word processing; and to my wife and family who have been very understanding when I have had to spend long hours at my desk.

PART

1

Making Sense

1

Making Sense

Walkers in Greenwich Park may at first be mystified by a line drawn across one of the footpaths. The line continues up the side of a house and across the middle of a window. Inside the window is an ancient telescope and on top of the house is a large ball on a pole. Once every twenty-four hours the ball is raised slowly and allowed to fall as the sun passes across the mid-line of the telescope at exactly 12 o'clock Greenwich Mean Time.

This is, of course, the Greenwich meridian from which degrees of longitude throughout the world are measured. It is in this particular spot simply because Charles II had a palace there, which included an observatory. In theory the reference line for longitude could have been anywhere in the world. In fact it happens to be in Greenwich for purely fortuitous reasons of history.

By contrast, travellers in Uganda may also encounter a line on a road and recognize it as the equator. The equator would be there whether the line existed or not, and in no sense depends on the line in the way that the Greenwich meridian does. On a sphere spinning on its own axis there is only one line at right angles to that axis representing the maximum circumference of the sphere. The position of the equator, therefore, is not the result of an accidental historical convention, but is inherent in the properties of a spinning globe, and is determined by the axis of rotation.

Longitude and latitude are thus different kinds of reference lines. The idea of dividing up the surface of a sphere in this way had to be invented, but the possibility of doing so is inherent in the shape of the sphere itself. The actual position of the lines on a rotating sphere is fixed by the properties of the sphere in the case of latitude, and arbitrarily chosen in the case of longitude.

The final choice of the Greenwich meridian was not made all at once and has a complex history. In the days before world travel nations tended to define longitude in relation to their own principal observatory. Cardinal Richelieu, for example, defined the French meridian as passing through Ferro in the Canary Islands on the grounds that this was the furthest accessible point west of Europe. Later this was redefined as being twenty degrees west of Paris. Standardization only became necessary with the growth of world travel, and since the best sea charts tended to be British the use of Greenwich as the reference line gradually spread. The process of standardization was further accelerated by the building of coast to coast railways in North America, which required travellers to pass through several time zones within fairly short periods. Agreements about world time depended upon agreements about longitude and so accelerated the move towards a single system. Greenwich was accepted internationally as the basis for this standardization in 1884 and only France maintained its own system before coming into line in 1911. One incidental advantage of the choice of Greenwich for the meridian is that the international dateline, which is its opposite number on the other side of the world, passes mostly through the Pacific Ocean.

The story of longitude and latitude can illustrate the rather complex relation between invention and discovery. Both have a basis in the way things are: in this instance in the mathematical properties of the surface of a sphere. But both concepts also needed to be invented in the sense that somebody had to think of dividing up the surface of a sphere by a system of co-ordinates. Once the concepts were invented, however, the equator could be found, together with all other degrees of latitude, purely by observing the position of the sun. The meridian, on the other hand, had to be deliberately chosen, and only when this choice was agreed could all other degrees of longitude be defined in relation to it. Neither latitude nor longitude was pure invention or pure discovery, but they differ significantly in the degree to which they disclose patterns already there in the way things are, or impose patterns as a result of conscious choice.

The distinction between them corresponds to two meanings of the phrase 'making sense'. Thus we can make sense, say, of a friend's peculiar behaviour on discovering that he has a splitting headache. What was previously puzzling becomes intelligible by the disclosure of previously unknown information.

In other circumstances it may be necessary to make sense of someone else's puzzling behaviour in a much more active and participatory way by changing our own attitude and behaviour towards them. The new understanding which can emerge out of this process does not lie in the discovery of something about our friend, which simply adds to a hitherto incomplete picture, but entails the creation of sense or meaning where incomprehension existed before. Forgiveness for a wrong done, for example, can create sense and meaning, by allowing the transformation of much that was previously hidden. New understanding flows from a new relationship.

Both these processes, the discovery of patterns of meaning and the creation of patterns of meaning, are familiar parts of ordinary thinking. Failure to appreciate the difference between them lies at the root of many disagreements, not least in theology. We can ask, for example, how far theological truth is simply 'given' and waiting to be discovered, or how far the actual form of theological statements depends on human creativeness and the accidents of history. I shall be suggesting throughout these chapters that both meanings of 'making sense' need to be borne in mind and related to one another, just as longitude and latitude belong within the same system of measurement but represent subtly different ways of representing geographical realities.

For the time being, however, I shall stick to science where the realist and instrumentalist interpretations correspond roughly to this distinction. In crude terms a realist view of science presupposes that science discovers what is in some sense 'really there', whereas an instrumentalist view envisages scientists as creating useful patterns of thought which give reliable results for certain limited purposes. Scientific theorems on this latter view are conceptual devices which are retained for as long as they work, but could have taken quite a different form had they arisen in different historical circumstances. Would Darwin's theory of natural selection, for instance, have been formulated with such a strong emphasis on struggle and competition if British society at the time had not itself been going through a social and economic revolution? Competition undoubtedly exists. In that sense there is a realist element in the theory. But since Darwin's day the simple conceptual scheme of competition between individuals for a limited food supply has had to give place to an enormously more sophisticated and complex model that draws insights from how modern societies interact. The borderline between realist claims about what actually happens, and constructions of reality which make sense in particular circumstances is a tricky one even in a broadly descriptive science like natural history.

A clearer example, though, of this interaction between the different ways of making sense is the classic case of Copernicus. The Copernican theory of the rotation of the earth round the sun could for a long time be treated as merely a useful, instrumentalist device which had the advantage of being conceptually simpler than the elaborate Ptolemaic system of concentric spheres and epicycles which then held sway. It was only when, in Galileo's time, the Copernican system began to be presented as 'really true' that opposition to it became fierce. In the eyes of the church authorities who condemned Galileo the threat posed by this new science was philosophical. Divergencies from Scripture could easily be explained away. A new conception of reality, however, reality as disclosed by science rather than as analysed by Aristotle and woven into theology, was a different matter altogether. Furthermore Galileo was already spelling out this new conception in a more detailed and precise way in his studies of matter and motion, and it would not be long before all reality was perceived in these mechanistic terms. Scientific realism, in other words, had implications for philosophy and theology which could not be ignored by those who hitherto had regarded science as producing no more than useful but limited hypotheses for strictly practical purposes.

With hindsight it is now possible to see that the protagonists on both sides were both right and wrong. Copernicus was right in a sense in which Ptolemy was not. Yet the Copernican and Newtonian models of the universe, which assumed a kind of fixed grid in space against which motion could be measured, have been turned on their head by Einstein. Following Einstein it is as if the universe's lines of longitude and latitude, far from being fixed, have all been revealed as arbitrary, merely relative to the point from which they are measured. Copernican realism, therefore, is not quite what it seems, though for many purposes it remains perfectly adequate. There is a proper sense in which it can be said that the earth goes round the sun, rather than vice versa, and space exploration would not have taken the form it has unless this were so. But the implications of relativity are more subtle. They only begin to impinge on most people's consciousness when astronomers talk of looking back into time through the observation of distant galaxies. The idea that we now see things which may long since have ceased to exist, can bring home the role that observation itself plays in our perception of what may seem to be really there. Few cosmologists these days can avoid the temptation to add philosophical epilogues to popular expositions of their science, thus unintentionally vindicating those philosophers and theologians of Galileo's time who were right to feel that what he was doing presented a challenge to their disciplines.

Galileo's other concerns, matter and motion, raised similar questions, though here the distinction between realism and instrumentalism is even harder to draw. What eventually became known as atomism presupposed that the universe really is made up of a finite number of discrete particles and that all observable phenomena can in the end be explained in terms of the interactions between these. It is a strongly compelling idea, and the realistic interpretation of it is made more convincing by the fact that under certain circumstances it is actually possible to see molecules. Our eyes thus seem to tell us that atoms are not useful explanatory devices, but must in some sense really exist. However this picture of real discrete particles becomes more confusing as more searching questions are asked about what they actually are. The deep structure of matter is not picturable at all. The very notion of some entity being at a particular place at a particular time and having a particular configuration breaks down at the sub-atomic level and much of classical physics has broken down with it. Even more disturbingly, the descriptions of what is observed at this deep level depend not just on what is there, but on the way in which the observations are made. Realism, in other words, gives way necessarily to instrumentalism. Making sense of sub-atomic phenomena has to include the acknowledgement that the observers themselves in part create the phenomena they observe.

Even clearer examples of the uncertain dividing line between what is really there and our descriptions of it are to be found in the psychological sciences where descriptions of phenomena depend hugely on the interpretative framework brought to bear on them. In what sense, for instance, does the Oedipus complex exist? Is there some real entity called intelligence which can be measured on a mathematical scale? Or are these simply useful fictions employed for particular and limited purposes?

The point at issue is simply that science at all levels moves between the two possible meanings of 'making sense'. There are patterns in nature waiting to be disclosed, and if there were not science would not be possible. There are also patterns in our minds which are to some extent imposed upon our experience, sometimes creating a kind of order that may hide a reality which is deeper and more mysterious. The severest critics of science go so far as to talk about it as a purely human construction. Feyerabend, for example, the best known philosopher of science who represents this extreme, refers to it as 'one of the many forms of thought which have been developed by man, and not necessarily the best'. He has not many followers. Most scientists, I believe, would think of themselves as 'critical realists'. They see their work as exposing patterns which are in a strong sense 'really there', though they would not wish to claim that these patterns are totally objective or that the full or final story has been told.

I have used these grossly over-simplified illustrations from science to make the point that the dual meaning of 'making sense' applies to all knowledge, including scientific knowledge. All knowledge is interpretation. The creative input into the interpretative process may vary widely from topic to topic and circumstance to circumstance. In our Western culture science was until recently regarded as the paradigm of knowledge, and the search for complete objectivity was the highest intellectual goal. Maybe it still is, and should be. But it is a goal which has to be pursued with a clear acknowledgement that it is in the end unattainable. Furthermore an understanding of the universe which leaves out the creative role of human consciousness within it is likely to be deficient compared with one which recognizes the subtle interplay between discovery and invention, observation and the use of the creative imagination.

The need to be aware of this interplay is even more obvious when thinking about the meaning of ordinary experience. Austin Farrer once described the various ways in which Mr Jones might make sense of his rheumatism. It is a condition which can, of course, be described medically, and part of the significance of labelling it 'rheumatism' is to relate it to similar sets of symptoms as recorded in fellow-sufferers. But this is not really how Mr Jones understands it himself. His own image of himself is as a patient sufferer enduring a 'trial'. Some of his acquaintances knowing how he behaves himself in his local pub are more inclined to think of his rheumatism as a punishment. However, when the bus carrying the annual British Legion outing turned over in a ditch, Mr Jones, who had been kept at home by his rheumatism, was happy to think of it as a blessing in disguise.

Meaning, in other words, depends upon context and on the kind of question being asked. Thus making sense of suffering may entail a whole range of approaches from looking into its causes, both immediate and remote, to the creative integration of it into life as a basis for deeper self-understanding, and as a spur to action. It can include everything from reductionist analysis to life-giving creativity and, as Mr Jones can remind us, there is room also for destructive interpretations as well as for fantasy. Nor are the different meanings necessarily mutually exclusive. Indeed suffering provides one of the clearest examples of how, on a personal level, realistic analysis and creative response can combine in ways which are profoundly integrative. A person suffering, say, from some disability may come to understand how and why it has been caused, perhaps by studying genetic linkages, but may also have gone beyond this understanding to a personal acceptance of the disability as setting parameters which he then sees as the spur to unique kinds of achievement. Such a person may make sense of it, in other words, both passively and actively. The disability may continue to be a huge source of frustration, and even at times despair, but in the context of a whole life it will be seen to have a meaning.

This search for sense and meaning, whether in the life of an individual, or in the vast panorama of scientific endeavour, does not appeal to everybody. In fact, one of the curiosities of the late twentieth century is the flight from sense and meaning in the so-called post-modernist movement with its deliberate challenge both to the idea that there is any sense inherent in the universe, and to the supposition that human beings might have a share in creating it. Any coherent attempt to represent the nature of the world or to act meaningfully within it must be either illusory or repressive. Reality is fragmentary, ephemeral, chaotic and discontinuous. Its perfect exemplar is television which hops from one image to another in the endless succession of change, and where all events are presented as having equal value, from a game show to a current affairs programme, and where the first criterion of success is the capturing of attention. The idea that one could make sense of a kaleidoscope is itself nonsensical, and although it might be possible to impose a meaning on a fleeting pattern of events or objects, this would not and could not be a sign of any meaning really there.

Not many people, I suspect, actually take post-modernism very seriously, and there are signs anyway that as a movement it has had its day. But fashionable movements have a trickle-down effect, and often find some echo in a less extreme but more widespread general feeling. The notion that there is sense to be made of the world, and of one's own life, has to struggle against a mood of unreflective individualism, a sense of a random element in experience and a suspicion of grandiose claims. The idea that meaning is important finds itself in competition with the belief that satisfaction is the immediate, and possibly the only, worthwhile goal. As a guide for life authorities which prescribe meanings are no longer trusted, and are under pressure to give place to open-ended discussion.

In setting out, therefore, to explore what it means to 'make sense' in a religious context I am conscious that there may be initial objections to the whole enterprise. Nevertheless, I hope those who have travelled thus far will judge, not on the basis of the preliminaries, but on whether sense actually emerges.

2

Making Sense of Faith

Despite its ambitious title my aim in this chapter is a modest one – to explore whether the relationship between invention and discovery can throw any light on the nature of Christian believing. Is faith a response to what is 'sheerly given', whether in biblical revelation or in the authoritative teaching of the Church, or in some combination of the two? Or is having faith an active process whereby believers make sense of their own lives, using materials provided from Christian sources, but fashioning them into something which is probably unique to the individual, in that it is shaped and coloured by individual experience?

This contrast is stated too sharply in that most people may find themselves somewhere between the two extremes. Nevertheless a look at the extremes may help in fixing our bearings.

Fundamentalism is nowadays the most vociferous form of the 'sheerly given' type of faith. Its stated aim is to return to the original sources of faith, freed from the accretions of history and clericalism, and to establish a direct relationship between the Word as embodied in Scripture and present-day experience. Even though history could provide such believers with lessons about how this process can become corrupted, by and large there is little sense of the historical development of faith, and the appeal in every circumstance of life is usually direct to Scripture.

14

The modern strength of fundamentalism lies in its claim to provide the only radical alternative to secularism. It does this by providing a key set of doctrines (the so-called 'fundamentals'), a source of authority uncontaminated by human traditions, and a complete guide to life in an inerrant book. Each of these claims needs further examination.

The fundamental doctrines – the divinity of Christ, his second coming, heaven and hell, substitutionary atonement, and the inspiration and authority of the Scriptures – were highlighted as a package by traditional evangelical groups in the United States in the period immediately before the First World War in response to the then popular modernist teachings. As individual doctrines they do, of course, have a long history before that, and each needs to be considered on its own merits. But as a package they were put together because they were clearly related to the assumptions and concerns of that period. The claim, therefore, that this particular package can somehow go behind history and stand above other traditions is falsified by its own history.

The claim to a source of authority uncontaminated by human traditions is equally dubious. Its attractiveness lies in the idea that it is possible to escape from the mess and muddle of ordinary human thinking by going straight to a divine teacher; all other claims to authority are caught in a vicious circle of relativism. The obvious problem with such a belief is that it seems to be falsified by the actual disagreements between different fundamentalist groups. Those who have a high and exclusive view of the authority of Scripture are no more immune than anyone else from the difficulties of actually interpreting it. The human factor inescapably enters in, whether it is recognized or not.

The hard core of fundamentalism is belief in the inerrancy of Scripture. Like Islam, it is the religion of a totally God-given book with no room for error except in the processes of transmission. It represents, albeit in a more vigorous form, what was the normal assumption which once underlay most Christian thinking, and was not a major issue before the rise of historical criticism in the mid-nineteenth century. All Scripture was regarded as authoritative, though it had to be understood in different ways, as history, poetry, allegory, moral guidance, etc. When historical criticism sharpened the issue, however, the choice which seemed to confront many believers was between treating the Bible as a literally true, significant and complete statement of the mind of God, or seeing it as a set of documents with a history needing to be read with the help of modern scholarship as belonging to its own time. It is not surprising that the choice seemed an agonizing one, and that the belief in inerrancy should gain harder edges as a protection against the erosive forces of modernism.

Unfortunately, in trying to protect the authoritativeness of revelation, the element of givenness within it was totally divorced from the human processes through which it had been received. Thus the Bible came to be seen, not as a human document at all, but as an encyclopaedia of factual information with no allowance made for the weaknesses, interests, and preconceptions of those who actually wrote it. It is regarded as literally out of this world, in a way which stands in sharp contrast to the claims made about Christ himself. But if belief about the Bible is to regain proper theological contact with belief about Christ then the principle of incarnation has to be taken seriously. Too much emphasis on divinity at the expense of humanity, too much emphasis on the revelation of timeless truths at the expense of real historical experience, distorts the relationship between God's activity and our human activity, which lies at the heart of Christian faith.

There is another unfortunate imbalance to which fundamentalism has led. Overemphasis on the Bible as a single book, all of which is revelatory to a greater or lesser degree, has led to uses of it which pay little attention to context. Deductions are made from texts, which assume that statements made in one context can be used to answer questions belonging to quite another. When Jesus refers, for instance, to Noah and Jonah, using Old Testament stories to make a point about his present hearers, he is clearly not doing so to give authoritative teaching about the historical reliability of the original stories. When the writer of 2 Timothy 3.16 refers to the inspiration of Scripture he can hardly be providing a proof text for the inspiration of our present Bible, which did not then exist. Not everything which may seem to follow logically from a particular passage of Scripture can be assumed to be part of the intended meaning of that passage. As a sheerly given type of faith, fundamentalism seems progressively to lose contact with the world of real people who 'saw, heard and touched the Word of life', and who can convey to us that authoritative vision, but did not shed their human limitations in so doing.

The opposite extreme to fundamentalism, a sheerly personal form of faith, is not so easy to describe coherently because it is of its very nature multifarious. Individualistic faiths are not totally invented. They tend to draw from a wide variety of sources on the pick and mix principle, and it is common for the different bits and pieces not to be brought together into any sort of unity. Surveys of popular religious belief frequently show up obvious inconsistencies, as when more people claim to pray than say they believe in a personal God.

A survey of mostly non-churchgoing young people's beliefs by the General Synod Board of Education undertaken in the mid-1970s revealed even then a widespread individualism in their approach to religion, a tendency which, according to the European Values survey, has become stronger in the last ten years. The actual contents of belief disclosed in the survey were a hotchpotch of images, some of them drawn from religious sources, many of them from popular science, but more from the 'science' of Dr Who than from the classroom, some from folk sayings and from popular culture. Nowadays television soap operas seem to play an important role in providing a quasi-mythological frame of reference within which viewers can locate their own responses.

The individualism has limits, though. The researchers commented:

> So long as people have group support or conventional, shared assumptions to make sense of their world, they seem able to tolerate without noticing them all sorts of hiatuses and contradictions. They behave in fact *as if* life were underpinned by beliefs but they do not work them out into coherent verbalized philosophies. In short *system*, if by that we mean a logically coherent pattern, may be exactly the wrong word to use of the phenomenon: it is more like a patchwork quilt or much-mended net than like a system. And it operates most of the time as an *implicit* attribution of 'sense' to the way things are in the world, and only very seldom orders itself into formal propositions about what

things 'mean' and why. Even when something approaching formal propositions has a part to play, it may not take the form of a consistent *single* system of meaning. It is well known that in milieux where there is a folk saying for every eventuality, these sayings often come in contradictory pairs: 'Him as asks don't get'; 'Him as don't ask, don't want'. Pragmatism and glaring inconsistency are hidden by the piecemeal application of whichever ready-made saying fits the particular case.

Making sense of life, therefore, at this extreme of individualism is by no means primarily an intellectual activity, nor is it purely solitary. It is, however, enormously vulnerable to changes of fashion, to loss of group support, and to issues and challenges which fall outside its very limited terms of reference. Fear of this vulnerability in a culture which seems to offer few firm supports and guidelines may be one of the factors which drives many young people into the arms of fundamentalism. A university chaplain writing about the doctrinal basis of university Christian Unions emphasizes the importance of self-discovery in the process of maturing, and comments:

> At a pastoral level, the doctrinal basis helps to create an important support group for people who are going through a period of rapid change. It is significant that when this immediate need falls away after their time in higher education, a large proportion of people move away from this style of faith and churchgoing, either to a new style or, more often than not, to no style whatsoever.[1]

Can we find a middle way between these extremes, a way in which both discovery and invention play their part?

There are, for instance, many non-fundamentalist and non-idiosyncratic ways of approaching the Bible. One possible approach looks for revelation by a rediscovery of the 'real' meaning of the text as intended and understood by those who first wrote and read it. The difficulty in this approach is that those who nowadays want to discover that meaning for themselves find themselves heavily dependent on scholarly analysis. Furthermore since scholars tend to disagree, the hunt is likely to be endless. I have earlier complained about fundamentalist inattention to context. The opposite fault is a scholarly obsession with context which renders the Bible virtually inaccessible to those non-scholars who nevertheless wish to do more than read it as if it were a contemporary document. It is a sad fact that scholarship, vital though it is, has made many people nervous about reading the Bible at all.

A second possible approach ignores all this, and does entail reading it as if it were a contemporary document. This is what happens in the typical parish Bible study group. Such groups are frequently quasi-fundamentalist, though without going all the way to belief in inerrancy. The expectation is that the Holy Spirit will enable the text to speak directly to the lives of those involved, and considerations of context, original meaning, and of the dangers of importing one's own meaning into the words, do not loom very large. The scene is set for this approach to the Bible by the regular reading of Bible passages in public worship, frequently without the benefit of explanation or interpretation. A large part of normal Christian consciousness is formed by well-remembered scriptural words lodged in the mind at their face value. The words of Jesus about divorce and non-violence, like the words of the prophets about poverty and injustice, are among those which still have this direct quality, and which over the centuries have shaped and challenged Christian behaviour.

But what about those direct sayings which now to many ears sound offensive, or no longer significant? How, without bringing in considerations of context and original meaning, can contemporary Christians respond to some of what St Paul says about women? If the Bible is not inerrant, how is it possible to distinguish timeless truth from socially conditioned error?

A more radical approach to the Bible sees it all as socially conditioned and belonging to a world which has now vanished. Without falling into the incoherent individualism described earlier, it creates its own interpretation drawing on the insights of contemporary culture. The story of the fall in Genesis 3, for instance, can be psychologized as a myth of adolescence. The resurrection, we can be told, is essentially about the discovery of new life here and now. The parable of the Good Samaritan, we have been confidently assured, is as much about the need to make sufficient money, as about then using it to provide for the needy.

Radical reinterpretation runs the constant risk of losing touch with the text itself. In the right hands it can be enormously stimulating and throw a flood of new light on sayings and stories which may have become stale through familiarity. But in the wrong hands it owes more to the interpreter than to the Bible.

I have done no more than sketch very briefly three among many possible ways of trying to make sense of the Bible. The systematic study of interpretation (hermeneutics) brings highly sophisticated insights to bear on the process. One of the fathers of modern hermeneutics, Hans-Georg Gadamer, described a kind of dialogue between text and interpreter. Truth, he said, comes to us as a disclosure; it speaks to us with its own power, and in so doing exercises a claim over us. Those who have allowed the Bible to speak to them directly will know what he means. But acceptance of that claim also depends on us, on who we are, what our experiences have been, how our attitudes have been predisposed, and so on. We all start as prejudiced observers, in the sense that when hearing or reading or experiencing anything we bring our own prior assumptions about what it is. We may approach a particular biblical passage, for example, as if it were history, or mythology, or liturgy, or fantasy, but must then allow the text itself to modify and correct those initial presuppositions.

So begins a dialogue between text and interpreter, in which both what is there in the text and what is brought to it by the interpreter are progressively integrated by self-criticism, by openness to what is given, by a readiness to learn from others, and by creative insight. What Gadamer is describing, in fact, is what I have called the dual process of making sense, both actively and passively, endeavouring to respond to what is really there, yet integrating it into life as it is actually lived, and so creating new understanding.

All this may seem a very complicated way of doing Bible study. It can seem less complicated if we envisage it as taking place, not through an individual interpreter, but through a communal tradition within which meanings progressively develop and in which individual believers can play their part, and receive what they need, without being too bemused by the scholarly ferment going on around them. It is important to shed the illusion that there is a single 'right' interpretation of the Bible. Each generation has read it in its own way, not crucially different from its predecessors, but bringing its own insights to make sense of it for its own world. There are central meanings which have stood the test of time, like the main tunnels in a colliery. There are also numerous lesser tunnels and coalfaces, some of which are no longer in use, and some of which are being worked without much prior notion of what they might yield. A mine, like a tradition, is a living growing entity, a product of human ingenuity, yet only meaningful because there is something really there to be mined.

What is true of the study of the Bible is true more generally of faith as a whole. Just as the Bible is not a single book with a single meaning, but a library of different insights and experiences capable of being interpreted in different ways, so the Christian faith has many dimensions and aspects. It contains historical claims which need to be evaluated. It presupposes a philosophical framework which is supportive of metaphysical claims about transcendent reality. It makes use of myths and stories to convey meanings which cannot easily be expressed in propositions. It is acted out in ritual and is known most fully in worship. It presents ethical demands. It is embodied in a community and conveyed through traditions which are the product of centuries of interpretation and interaction. A mature faith, in other words, provides a complex cultural context within which believers think and act and live out their lives. It can enable those who belong to it to discover an order and meaning in their experience of the world, and also to impose an order and meaning upon it. It is a social matrix for the kind of dialogue with what is given, which Gadamer described as the process of interpretation. Christian faith centred on the cross and resurrection has a unique capacity to create meaning out of apparent meaninglessness.

Thirty years ago, in writing about the kind of spiritual emptiness which a hard-line scientific interpretation of the world can sometimes provoke, I used sacramental theology as an example of the creation of meaning:

Those who take Jesus Christ, rather than the world of nature, as the starting point of their search for God may find the world no less empty than their atheist or agnostic colleagues. However, for them this is not an invitation to despair but a programme for action. The God who is found supremely in one human life must be sought in faint reflection in every human life. The God who made one human life supremely meaningful can make every human life meaningful. The God who used the ordinary stuff of human life as the means by which He revealed Himself can make the ordinary world serve His purposes. But He does all this by inviting disciples, by winning men's co-operation, rather than by forcing a pattern upon events. Perhaps Nietzsche was right when he said that what meaning there is in the world, we create for ourselves; but I believe he was wrong when he described such creation as arbitrary. Those who take their starting point in Christ find themselves commissioned to make sense of their experience, as He made sense of it, by using it for God.

This is one of the ways of understanding the Christian sacraments. The characteristic method of Christian worship is to take bits of the ordinary stuff of life, bread and wine and water, and raise them to a new level of significance. The action is not arbitrary; the sacraments are what they are because they stem from Christ; they are 'given'. But once given, the sacramental principle can be extended to the whole of nature. Natural things can be consciously clothed with a new meaning by relating them to Christ. The world, which would be meaningless by itself, becomes a purposeful place as men make it so; and they are enabled to do this because they themselves find a purpose for their lives in the man whose life was wholly one with God.

A Christian who thinks like this can then see his vocation as an active process of 'making sense' of the world. This is different from the passive attempt to make sense of things, i.e. to understand them. The Christian attitude is to ask what we ought to make of them, what their possibilities are in a world responsible to God, how far they can be made the grounds of worship and thanksgiving. Scientific under- standing has an important part to play in this process, because religion is always in danger of degenerating into fancifulness, and grasping its satisfactions too cheaply. But scientific understanding by itself is only half the story. Knowledge must not be thought of as something detached from persons who know and act. Science searches for impersonal knowledge; Christianity insists that knowledge carries responsibilities, and that we only know the world truly as we use it rightly for God.[2]

It will be obvious from this that my basic beliefs have not changed much in thirty years. The last sentence of that quotation could lead straight to a theology of the environment, which was hardly appearing over the horizon when the words were written. The sacramental emphasis could be supplemented by the now familiar idea of human beings as co-workers with God. I am less impressed by Nietzschean meaninglessness today than I was then. But the basic point that we know, not only by observing, but by acting, is as old as religion itself. As we shall see in Chapter 3, it provides the clue to the meaning of prayer.

Notes

1. *Theology* (December 1992), p. 440.
2. J. Habgood, *Religion and Science* (Mills & Boon 1964), pp. 149–50.

3

Making Sense of Prayer

There are some contexts in which prayer comes naturally even to people who would not think of themselves as the praying type. Most people pray when they are afraid, or when they face bereavement. There are prayers which grow out of a gnawing sense of anxiety, prayers which verge on superstitious incantations to keep some loved person safe. There are also spontaneous prayers of praise and thanksgiving, from a simple 'Thank God' to a much more deliberate acknowledgement of what has somehow been given. The sophisticated may find themselves in trouble here. Katherine Mansfield once lamented when visiting the Alps: 'If only one could make some small grasshoppery sound of praise to someone, thanks to someone – but who?'

At the other end of the scale there are those for whom all kinds of prayer in all kinds of circumstances are unproblematic. They live by simple trust. They feel God close to them as a conversation partner, and no questions are asked about what is actually happening. Prayer at the intuitive stage of faith, the stage usually associated with children, has this quality. A more conventional adult faith, which has not been critically related to the remainder of life, may also find prayer unproblematic; it is done because it has always been done, and analysis would be out of place. Recent years have seen a huge upsurge in a different kind of simple faith, a faith which needs ask no

24

questions because answers to prayer are all around it. Much popular evangelical literature is packed with anecdotes witnessing to the belief that a praying life is a life full of miracles. My favourite is the story of the clergyman who claimed that God always found him a parking place when he drove to London because, in the knowledge that he was a bad driver, it was important to get him off the road as soon as possible.

There are also some types of prayer which are unproblematic because the changes wrought by them may be seen as solely in the minds of those who pray. Prayer as a process of self-discovery makes no metaphysical claims about God, and the results of it can be evident in terms of a more integrated personality and greater self-acceptance. The prayer of submission to the will of God is likewise directed inwards and no questions need to be asked about what it actually does, except to the person concerned. Meditation and adoration focus an attitude towards God and heighten awareness of God, but it is perhaps significant that meditative techniques are now widely practised by those who do not specifically link meditation with prayer at all. The summit of adoration, the prayer of silence, in one sense costs 'not less than everything', but raises few intellectual problems. Silence before ultimate mystery needs no justification.

There are many respects, therefore, in which making sense of prayer may seem like an unnecessary exercise. Yet for most people such a dismissal of problems would fail to get to the heart of the matter. Unless prayer can somehow be seen as related to God's activity in the world, much of what has been traditionally meant by it is in danger of becoming vacuous. The question insistently asked is, does prayer make a difference? To answer simply in terms of anecdotes is not enough. Making sense of prayer, like making sense of the sacraments, needs some insight into what, so far as we can tell, is actually going on. It needs also an awareness of our own role in creating a new reality through the act of praying.

The intellectual difficulties in conceiving God's action in the world do not derive primarily from science. Science has disclosed the orderliness of the universe, but only by first assuming it. The most successful sciences have won their laurels by studying those aspects of experience which are most amenable to this kind of ordering. The human and social sciences, usually regarded as poor relations by those who work in the natural sciences, struggle to find orderly and reliable patterns in human affairs, and their degree of success can be not unfairly measured by, say, the extent of the agreement among economists about what is best for the British economy. Even in the natural sciences, however, there is a growing recognition that the full story has not, and cannot, be told. The universe has revealed itself this century as much more open-textured, much less rigidly determined, than the classical scientists of the previous two centuries supposed. It is now seen that scientific study may have tried to impose an order on phenomena which in the end prove not to be so tightly circumscribed. The result of all this has been to make scientists much less dogmatic about what can or cannot happen. It can be argued convincingly that in theory there is no reason why some special activity by God need not be a feature of the way the universe functions. In the actual practice of science, however, such ideas are almost invariably ruled out as having any part to play in scientific investigation, because to invoke divine causality for events is to bring further questioning to a halt. Science and thoughts of divine activity, therefore, do not easily mix. But science by itself does not forbid an understanding of the universe in which prayer might make a difference.

The problem of God's activity in an orderly universe is more a moral one than a scientific one. Belief in an orderly universe is a necessary basis for responsible behaviour. It is only as people believe that there is a more or less consistent relationship between actions and their consequences that moral action becomes possible. In a chaotic society individual moral behaviour counts for less and less, at least in the immediate situation. Alice trying to play croquet in Wonderland with a flamingo as mallet and hedgehogs as balls found the game impossible because nothing kept still. A world in which the rules could be changed or suspended at the request of billions of people saying their prayers would lack all moral consistency. It might be possible in theory to imagine God as orchestrating a billion responses to prayer, but without some fixed rules of orchestration most events would be seen as arbitrary and unrelated. Competing prayers in wartime have often been used to illustrate the essential moral problem. A poem written at the time of the First World War neatly summed it up:

> To God the embattled nations sing and shout:
> 'Gott strafe England' and 'God save the King',
> 'God this, God that, and God the other thing'.
> 'Good God', said God, 'I've got my work cut out.'

A further moral dilemma created by belief in effective prayer centres on the prayers which are not answered. What kind of a world is it in which God can supposedly find parking spaces for clergymen, yet fail to answer the prayers of six million Jews going to their deaths in Hitler's Germany? What seems morally offensive in many of the claims about answered prayer is their triviality in comparison with the monstrous evils which are faithfully laid before God by millions of praying people every day, seemingly without much effect. It is the same disproportion which makes supposed communications with the dead through spiritualism so unconvincing. If life after death is really so drably suburban, heaven hardly seems worth worrying about.

It can be answered that it is not God's way to eradicate monstrous evils other than through suffering love. Horrors can be redeemed, redeemed often through prayer, by deliberately making sense of them in an act of self-offering. This is not the same as the discovery of a meaning which is already there in something which seems essentially meaningless, but entails the creation of meaning through reinterpretation. The famous prayer found in Ravensbruck concentration camp is a profound and moving example of such a response:

> O Lord, remember not only the men and women of good will but also those of ill will. But do not only remember the suffering they have inflicted on us; remember the fruits we bought, thanks to this suffering, our comradeship, our loyalty, our humility, the courage, the generosity, the greatness of heart which has grown out of all this, and when they come to judgement, let all the fruits which we have borne be their forgiveness.

I shall be returning to this idea of creative reinterpretation towards the end of this chapter. Meanwhile there is a need to look more closely at what the concept of God's action in the world actually means, and whether it is necessarily bound up with the disruption of physical and moral orderliness, that make it objectionable in the eyes of some.

Our starting point must be the Bible, because it is the biblical notion of the God who acts, that underlies this whole discussion. Even a quick glance at the Bible, however, reveals that the concept is not a simple one, and that God's perceived mode of action is by no means always the same. For convenience, I shall group different examples under four headings:

1. Providential Oversight

The Joseph saga (Genesis 37—50) is the classic instance of a story which can be read and understood in purely secular terms, and which reveals its theological significance only in the final dénouement. At first sight it is about brotherly treachery and Joseph's revenge. But with hindsight it is seen quite differently. 'You meant it for evil, but God meant it for good' (Genesis 50.20). Through these sordid events God has been working his providential purpose to save Israel. The Book of Esther at a much later period in history exemplifies the same point.

Secular history, on this view, is not disrupted by God, but used by him. What the believer brings to it is an interpretation which reveals its true significance. The problem from the believer's point of view is to know what events are to be interpreted in this way, and what interpretation is to be placed on them. The evacuation of Dunkirk in 1940, for instance, was widely interpreted as a miracle at the time, and this belief was a large factor in sustaining British morale when it could have cracked altogether. Confusingly, though, Hitler's escape in the bomb plot of 1944 was also widely interpreted, not least by himself, as a miracle, a belief which probably lengthened the war. Both events emerge as much more ambivalent in the light of subsequent history. Indeed from a secular perspective the idea of 'the true significance' of an event is a difficult one to sustain. The moral seems to be that the discernment of providential oversight is full of pitfalls, at least as dependent on the interpretative framework brought to bear on events as on the events themselves.

2. Prophetic Fulfilment

This concept provides the backbone of the historical narratives of the Old Testament, and the essential link between the Old and the New. There is a repeated pattern of prophecies which give significance to special events, which then become the basis for further prophecies and further fulfilments. The way in which the exodus of Israel from Egypt is used to interpret the return of the Jews from exile in Babylon, which in turn provides the imagery of suffering and renewal used to interpret the resurrection, is perhaps for Christians the central strand of biblical prophecy. In this mode of representing God's activity it is not just that the interpretations of events are shaped by expectations, but that the events themselves are brought about in large part because people believe the promises concerning them. This was certainly true of the return of the Jews from exile. It was not true, however, of the resurrection nor of the prophecies concerning the Messiah, where the fulfilment of prophecy went beyond what had been promised and thus, while dependent initially on an interpretative framework, also had the effect of reshaping it.

3. The Divine Programme

The apocalyptic literature in the Bible (Daniel and parts of Ezekiel, Revelation and passages like Mark 13) poses particular problems about the nature of God's activity, because in these his action seems to follow a set course, laid down long in advance and carried through programmatically irrespective of human response. The programmes contain precise timings which have proved to be a happy hunting ground for over-ingenious interpreters ever since. The assumption underlying apocalyptic is that history is deterministic, an assumption which not only undermines the moral worth of human actions but fits uneasily with the assumption underlying prophecy, namely that an appropriate response can change the future.

My own belief is that apocalyptic literature, valuable though it is in providing inspiration, is in the end incompatible with the remainder of the Bible and with beliefs about the open-ended character of the universe. It springs from a distorted emphasis on God's sovereignty, built up under the pressure of extreme circumstances, when those who were suffering saw no hope other than in a supernatural overriding of history by an all-powerful God. It should not, in my view, be used as a reliable model of the way God actually works.

4. Signs and Wonders

There are plenty of stories of signs and wonders in the Old Testament. Moses, Elisha and Daniel perform spectacular feats as evidence of the power of God at work in them, some of which, particularly Elisha's, seem oddly inconsequential to modern eyes. The miraculous element in these stories clearly implies direct supernatural intervention. They are wonders rather than signs.

By contrast the miracles of Jesus are for the most part presented as deliberately low-key. The emphasis is on signs rather than wonders, and even the signs are to be used sparingly. St John's Gospel, while containing some of the most spectacular accounts of miracles, is at most pains to interpret them as signs of deeper truths about Jesus himself. The notion of God's intervention is not primarily used as evidence of his power, but becomes more and more focused on Jesus' own coming.

Three broad principles seem to emerge from this quick glance at different ways in which God's activity is represented in the Bible. First there is the general belief that God is indeed active in the world as the ground of all historical events, but faith is needed to perceive it. Secondly, the response of faith can actually make a difference to what happens, and in this sense God can be said to act in the world through the evocation of faith in believers. Thirdly, there are some events, particularly those associated with key religious figures, which have an exceptionally striking character and are seen as uniquely revealing of God's activity.

Building on these principles, it is not necessary to confine the notion of God's activity simply to events described in the Bible. The Bible is, as it were, a window on the world, a revelation in concrete historical terms of what is claimed to be universally true. Just as the story of Joseph can be read in secular terms and also as a demonstration of providential care, and just as it is possible to describe the world as God's creation and also as the product of a cosmological process, so it may be possible to read all history both as a network of cause and effect and as the arena of God's action.

In such a world prayer could be a channel of contact with this hidden dimension of God's activity. It could illuminate with meaning the life of those who pray. It could open the way to all sorts of responses of faith which might themselves help to change the world. But this picture does not yet enable us to see how prayer might in some more direct sense make a difference. Even though everything is part of God's activity, the question still remains whether some things are part of his activity in a special way which may fall outside the normal pattern of things. And if so is it possible to make sense of the idea? To put the point more crudely, should twentieth-century Christians still expect miracles?

At this stage in the argument it may be helpful to use an analogy from human action. Without going into complex discussions about free will, I am going to take for granted the paradox that, while all our human mental processes depend on physical and chemical interactions in our brains which are in principle capable of being explained, human beings can nevertheless make free choices. How this is possible, nobody knows. But it is a fact of experience, and it accords with what was said earlier about the open texture of the universe. Human free will is the clearest example of how it is possible to have a law-abiding universe in which, despite its overall regularities, some events are unpredictable. Never mind for a moment what God does. Human creativity can and does make a difference.

In exploring this theme of human free will Austin Farrer once drew a nice distinction between predictability and dependability:

The Parry-Joneses come to call. We rely on Uncle Peter and Cousin George to rise to the occasion. There are many things we are sure they will not do. They will not talk across to one another, and ignore the Joneses. They will not go on reading 'Country Life' and the 'Sporting Times'. They will not insult the Welsh character. But these are negatives. What will they do? Our reliance on them to act characteristically may involve very different expectations: about Uncle Peter the sickening certainty that he will tell the anecdote of the two Irishmen; about Cousin George, that he will sum up his company in the twinkling of an eye, draw them out, pick up the points of their interest, and lead them on into one of those charming conversational games, in the invention of which he has an inexhaustible fertility. In fact, we rely on Uncle Peter to do, alas! exactly what we expect; and with an equal confidence we rely on Cousin George to do what we don't expect. Our expectation in the one case fills in the whole picture; in the other it defines the merest frame, with 'something ingenious and polite' written under it.[1]

On the basis of this distinction we can identify two elements in human activity which I shall call regularity and surprise. The question then arises whether God relates to his creation in a way which also contains these two elements. The regularity, the dependability is, as I have already said, an essential basis for believing that this is a world in which responsible behaviour is possible. The mapping of the regularities is the job of science. There may also be room for surprise, not chaotic surprise, but as in Cousin George, an outflow of endless dependable creativity.

Surprise is, of course, a relative term. What surprises one person may not surprise another. What is surprising in one age may be viewed quite differently in the next. But surprises when they come tend to be revealing, both in relation to the events themselves and in relation to those who are surprised. The moment of surprise is one in which the boundaries between ourselves and the world of events grow thinner and more transparent.

The same could be said of miracles. To those who perceive them they are God's surprises. But not everyone perceives them in the same way. Yesterday's miracle may be tomorrow's medical platitude, but this need in no way lessen the genuine gratitude and sense of God's graciousness which a surprise cure evokes. Those who see miracles everywhere are those who expect them. Too much emphasis on the miraculous may devalue the currency and lead to a certain naivety about what can be known and what cannot. But for the purposes of prayer the important thing is to recognize God as in everything, whether in the regularities or in the surprises. A definition of miracle, which I believe gets the balance about right, is that it is a surprising event which strikes those who witness it with the force of a revelation from God. The essence of miracle lies in the combination of event and interpretation.

Some events, of course, would be surprising in any context. The central miracle of the resurrection falls into this category. But the point needs to be made again that for even such a stupendous event as this to be recognized as a revelation from God, the ground had to be prepared. The recognition was possible because the disciples had the theological understanding they needed to interpret what had happened. Without the framework of faith, even the most profound and dramatic of signs is reduced to a mere wonder, or dismissed as impossible.

Against this background what sense can now be made of prayer? It is not to be seen as petitioning a law-giver to break his own rules. Rather it is the encountering of a personal dependable reality, hearing, knowing, loving and surprising.

This involves discovery. It is a response to real events, interpreted by faith. The events may be highly specific, experiences which seem to shout that here is a moment of decision, a challenge, a revelation. Or they may be quite general, a sense of the meaningfulness of life, a thanksgiving for life itself. Some events may be interpreted only in retrospect as means by which God has led us. Providential care is usually apparent only in the long view. Sometimes it may be an absence of experience, a hanging on in the dark, when it has to be accepted in faith that there *is* a meaning in what is happening to us, even if it cannot be seen. Some significant events and experiences are simply discarded because those concerned have no language for them, no context in which their significance can be properly grasped. Recent studies of religious experience have revealed a huge reservoir of potential religious awareness in people who through lack of contact with actual religions have no means of expressing it.

Prayer also involves invention or creation. It is the making sense of life by the deliberate claiming of its different aspects for God. It is the conscious harnessing of the freedom given to human beings to create their own meaning, and the conscious recognition that this freedom exists only in relation to the freedom of God.

The traditional elements of prayer can be described in these terms. Thanksgiving is a way of saying, 'I need not have been given this, yet I was'. In not taking things for granted it acknowledges God's freedom to give or withhold and our freedom to receive or not to receive. Thanksgiving, in other words, acknowledges and enlarges the area of free inter-change between ourselves and God.

Penitence and the acknowledgement of responsibility do the same. In effect the penitent is saying, 'I need not have done this, yet I did'. To shuffle off responsibility is to deny our freedom and to diminish ourselves as human beings. Penitence, entailing the acceptance of responsibility and all that follows from it, enables the personality to grow.

Expressions of hope and fear when laid before God carry the message, 'I am not bound by seeming inevitabilities'. Despite promises or threats the future remains open. Prayers of longing and commitment assert a faith in the possibilities of self-transcendence: 'I am not bound by my present condition'.

Intercession is a claiming before God of this same openness for the futures of others. It is an affirmation that freedom is indivisible, and that persons and the possibilities open to them inextricably belong to each other. Intercessory prayer has often been likened to a releasing of the grace of God in the lives of those being prayed for. God, as it were, needs our responsiveness in order to act, because he acts always with the forbearingness of love. This responsiveness is not merely individual. The more we strengthen the links of sympathy and understanding with each other through prayer, the greater the scope for love to do its work. From the human side, what I have described as the enlarging of the area of personal freedom before God might be seen as having the same effect. From God's side, the old adage about God always hearing prayers but answering them in his own – sometimes surprising

- way, asserts God's own freedom on which ours depends. It may also be true that God exercises his freedom mainly by working through people whose own openness to him allows things to happen.

If this understanding of prayer as the enlargement of the area of free responsible relation between God and humanity carries conviction, then the main difference prayer makes lies in satisfying humanity's greatest need, our need of God himself. George Macdonald made the point succinctly: 'Hunger may drive the runaway child home, and he may or may not be fed at once, but he needs his mother more than his dinner.'

Note

1. Austin Farrer, *The Freedom of the Will* (A. & C. Black 1958), p. 166.

4

Making Moral Sense

The idea that morality might owe much to human invention rather than being simply 'given' might seem subversive. Surely the whole point of moral demands is that they exert a claim on us. They are there, and we come up against them, and our lives are shaped by the way we respond to them. Self-chosen moral standards, or worse, self-invented ones, lack the essential element of constraint, or of the imperative, which together make morality what it is.

The accusation of subversiveness has force. Yet it is obvious that the simple contrast between given standards and invented ones fails to do justice to the complex process by which they come to be. Morality, like prayer, is a mixture of response to what is given and the exercise of human creativity.

Each of us, for example, is born and brought up in a particular culture which consciously or unconsciously provides us with our initial moral standards. We feel strongly about cruelty to animals, say, because we live in a society where pets are common and where social attitudes encourage us to empathize with some, but not all, animals, and where abattoirs are mostly kept out of sight. The sense that kindness to animals is morally 'given' can be seen to arise from the fact that it is assumed as part of our cultural heritage. If we had been born, for example, in Turkey where sheep are openly sacrificed in the streets, or in Spain where horrible things may be done to animals as part of local Christian festivals, we might think differently.

Thus far the givenness can be seen as a culturally conditioned givenness, as one invented or developed within a particular society, and not as a givenness which somehow belongs to the nature of things. But can we go further than this? Can we say that a culture which is kind to animals is somehow better than a culture which is cruel to them? And if so, on what grounds?

The fact is that people do criticize other cultures, including their own, in ways which go beyond saying, 'This is the way I do things, and I want you to conform to it'. The appeal to moral standards is in the end an appeal to something which is held to be universally true. Cruelty to animals, it is claimed, is wrong wherever it happens, because cruelty of any kind is wrong. There may be differences of opinion about precisely what constitutes cruelty, but the motive which drives English ladies to rescue injured cab-horses in Cairo is seen as a response to a fundamental moral imperative which transcends their cultural background. If it is still argued that moral imperatives are no more than the products of particular cultures, then ask whether the culture which produced Auschwitz should be judged by its own standards or by standards of right and wrong which lay outside it.

But if there is a givenness in morality which is not simply the result of cultural conditioning, where is it to be found? Conscience cannot be the answer because conscience has to be educated, and in any case much of its education will be culturally influenced. Reason may be part of the answer, but we shall encounter some of the problems associated with that a little later. The most common religious answer to the question is, of course, that moral standards are rooted in the will of God, but even that has difficulties. In the biblical tradition these are brought to the surface most sharply in the Book of Job. The problem Job wrestles with in the midst of his suffering is whether it is possible to criticize God for being unjust. He believes passionately that what has happened to him far exceeds anything he could possibly have deserved. Yet on what grounds is it possible to accuse God except by standards of justice derived from God himself? A somewhat similar conundrum has been set out in a much more modern question on which a great deal of ink has been spilt. Is something right simply because God says it is? Or is there a sense in which something can be said to be good inherently, and which might be used as a basis for criticizing, if not God himself, at least certain concepts of God? When one thinks of the cruelties perpetrated throughout history in the name of God, the questions have some point. To begin to answer them, though, requires a closer look at the senses in which moral standards may be said to be 'given'.

The most extreme form of givenness is found in the notion of law by divine fiat – or arbitrary law, as it is often termed. Right and wrong are defined by reference solely to a body of law which needs no justification beyond the fact that it has been given by God. Considerable sections of Old Testament law have this character. The law is simply stated and is there to be obeyed. Ingenious interpreters may work out its practical implications in highly elaborate schemes, but the law itself remains the bedrock on which a whole way of life may depend.

One of the oddest of such laws is found in Exodus 23.19: 'Thou shall not seethe a kid in its mother's milk'. Nothing is really known of its origins. Perhaps it refers to some long-forgotten practice, maybe to the rejection of some Canaanite fertility rite. But accepted without explanation as a command of God, it has become the basis of a complete culture which profoundly affects the life of every orthodox Jew. Meat and milk may not be eaten at the same meal. So absolute is the separation between them that different utensils are used for anything to do with meat and for any milk product. Large houses may even have two kitchens, one for meat and one for milk. And all this is based on a strange little law which may once have made good sense but is now accepted in its arbitrariness.

Some years ago after experiencing this prohibition at first hand in Israel I asked a highly intelligent modern young Israeli how he could justify it to himself. His answer was, 'If God only asked us to do things which were sensible and rational it would make no difference to us whether we believed in him or not. But because he asks us to do something which is patently irrational, we remember him at every meal.' In a word, the religious significance of arbitrary law lies precisely in its arbitrariness. Belief in this extreme form of givenness has become part of belief in God.

The repeated emphasis in many Christian circles on the

absoluteness of moral laws springs from the same religious insight. And not only in Christianity. For Muslims the Koran is simply given. Any defect or deviation would destroy it.

To be religiously significant, however, moral laws do not necessarily have to be arbitrary. They can be seen to make sense at a deeper level than that of rational calculation. The Sermon on the Mount, for instance, is not rational. Yet, equally, it is not arbitrary in the sense in which some of the Old Testament laws seem to be arbitrary. It touches deep chords in those who hear it and evokes the response that this is what real human life is all about. As a blueprint for living it may only be practicable, and hardly even then, in extreme circumstances, say, within a religious community. Yet it has inspired centuries of Christian devotion, heroism and self-sacrifice. It has done this, however, mostly by haunting Christian consciences, and only in individual cases by prescribing precise rules about how Christians should behave.

Here, then, is another kind of givenness, a givenness which makes itself felt through capturing the imagination. Reinhold Niebuhr coined the phrase, 'the relevance of an impossible ethical ideal'. He used it to sum up the need both to acknowledge the uncompromising demands of love and to accept the limitations of human finiteness. The Sermon on the Mount brings us face to face with both.

A third type of givenness can be found in a religiously based morality which can at the same time appeal to reason, and may thus be applicable both to believers and to non-believers. Most of the Ten Commandments, for example, make good sense in a secular environment, as well as carrying high religious authority. It is possible to argue about their origin and meaning, and not hard to see their relevance in the kind of society in which they originated. The fact that they are still so relevant says something about the continuities of human life and culture. Whether appeal is made to their rationality or to their authority is likely to depend on circumstances.

A further step down this road towards reason-based religious morality is the natural law tradition which has looked for moral givenness in analysis of the givenness of nature, especially human nature. The underlying assumption has been that it is possible by careful inspection, philosophical and scientific, to decide what the aim and function of various natural processes should be within the purposes of God, and that this should then determine the moral conditions for their use. It is fairly easy, for instance, to agree that human beings need to eat, and to deduce from this a moral imperative about the just distribution of food. It is less easy to agree on the precise use of the reproductive organs, and it is noteworthy that although the Roman Catholic prohibition of contraception is ostensibly based on natural law, it was in practice backed up and enforced by the invocation of papal authority.

It is clear, then, that despite its huge advantages in promising a universal basis for morality, the natural law tradition is not without its difficulties. These have been compounded in this century by the virtual breakdown of the concept of nature itself. The tradition assumed a relatively static world in which things were what they were, and had received a fixed nature and constitution from the hand of God. In a fluid, open-textured and evolving world, that picture is immeasurably more complicated. The tradition is having to adapt to new realities and, if it is to continue to provide the basis for moral givenness, it seems likely that it is going to have to rely more and more on a theological undergirding, which takes much more account of the present degree of fluidity and pluralism within theology itself.

Against that trend it is important to note the real degree of convergence on some basic moral principles among peoples of different faiths and cultures. Whether this is due to cultural mixing, or to a growing awareness that certain conditions are necessary for living a decent human life, is hard to say. Nevertheless the fact that it has been possible for so many diverse countries to reach agreement on basic human rights is surely significant. These do not go anything like as far as the natural law tradition tried to go, but they point to a givenness in the human condition which may to some degree provide a broadly acceptable basis for a secular morality.

Attempts to base morality on reason alone represent the fourth and final type of givenness to be considered. This was the Enlightenment ideal, a rejection of religious moral authority and its replacement by a rational morality based on scientific insight into 'the nature of man'. This may look like a repeat of the natural law tradition, but whereas the religious moralists looked at humanity as it should be in the purposes of

God, the Enlightenment moralists set out to look at humanity as an object of scientific study. The difficulty which soon emerged is that science is at its most ineffective in the study of human nature because what is most distinctive of human beings systematically eludes scientific categorization. To be human is to live with a sense of incompleteness. We do not even know ourselves. How then can the essence of being human be objectivized and universalized by reason?

Moralists standing in the Enlightenment tradition, from Kant through the utilitarians to the modern surfeit of psychological and sociological prescriptions, have done their best, all purporting to tell us what is good for us. Others like Nietzsche have faced the dilemma, pronounced the failure of reason, and proclaimed a morality which is pure invention. Man, according to Nietzsche, creates himself, and the strong man imposes his will on the others.

In his seminal book, *After Virtue*, Alasdair MacIntyre has pronounced the death of this tradition. Reason by itself cannot provide a basis for morality, and the conclusive evidence for this is that the protagonists of an exclusively rational morality have never in fact been able to agree. Indeed reason itself can only operate within a tradition of thought which itself has a history, and belongs within a culture in which much is already accepted as given.

There is no escape, therefore, from at any rate some degree of circularity in our attempts to make moral sense. The search for the source of the given element in morality leads us back again and again to religious belief as the bedrock on which it is based.

But religious belief itself may need to be open to moral criticism. Gods can easily become tyrants unless there is feedback from moral insights to the contents of belief itself. Arbitrary law, while capable of high religious value, can have a correspondingly low moral value. The Book of Job is one of the high points of the Old Testament precisely because it goes beyond the received tradition in its moral criticism of conventional religion, yet ends with a deeper insight into the faith which it had rejected. Job, who is shown in page after page as complaining against God, challenging him, pleading with him and cursing him, at last encounters him at a depth which both vindicates the traditional theology of his friends, and shows up its shallowness.

Christian morality finds its ultimate givenness in Christ. Yet how to translate that givenness into actual prescriptions for behaviour has been a constant problem for Christian interpreters. The difficulties in knowing how to respond to the Sermon on the Mount have already been mentioned. How far the actual teaching of Jesus, say on the subject of divorce, should be seen in its historical context and interpreted differently in our very different social circumstances, is another problem already considered in Chapter 2. There are far bigger issues, however, which centre on the interpretation of the meaning of the cross, and which take us back to the kind of paradoxes expressed in Job. If redemption comes through the suffering of injustice, what does this tell us about Christian engagement in the struggles against injustice which are seen to be so urgently necessary in today's world?

The unfolding of the deeper implications of the cross of Christ has been a constant preoccupation of theologians and moralists throughout Christian history. The only point I am concerned to make about it here is that its moral meaning cannot simply be read off from the facts themselves. The givenness of the cross acts as a reference point against which human attempts to make sense of our condition have to be judged; but it is a reference point which does not itself provide unambiguous answers.

Moral inventiveness is in any case necessary. Human circumstances are always changing, and our age has to an unparalleled extent had to face the moral implications of new knowledge, new techniques, new possibilities of choice and new dangers of self-destruction. Some of the other chapters in this book illustrate my own efforts to tackle some of these issues on the basis of Christian insight. This can be a risky and controversial business, but controversy between Christian thinkers is not necessarily to be deplored. Insofar as making moral sense is a creative and not merely a deductive activity, the conflict of opinions may be just what is needed to sift the good from the bad.

Expanding Belief

Sermon preached in York Minster, Christmas Day 1992

Anyone who has been to Bethlehem will know the famous door at the entrance to the Church of the Nativity. It is so low that you practically have to crawl through it. The story is that it was made that way when there was a fear that marauding horsemen might ride into the church and kill the worshippers. Nowadays it has a different meaning. It has come to symbolize the only way to approach the great mystery of the incarnation – on one's knees.

Last summer I encountered a similar doorway when staying in an African roundhouse. In fact I encountered it with my head every time I went in. The architectural reason for having a very low door in a house which is virtually a hemisphere is fairly obvious: a high door would let in the rain. But once again this door had been given a symbolic meaning; those who approach the owner of a house do so humbly, as suppliants.

This adding of new depths of meaning to something which might have had quite simple origins, can be seen at work in our celebration of Christmas. Critical commentators these days are never tired of pointing out that December 25 is an old Roman feast-day marking the rebirth of the sun after the shortest day of the year, and adapted for Christian use. Most of the ceremonies we nowadays associate with Christmas are late in origin, some of them medieval, many of them Victorian. Does it matter? Not at all. It is what Christmas Day means for us now which matters. If our celebrations are true to the central message that God so loves us that he has shared our humanity in Jesus Christ, then all the other Christmas things can fall into place round this.

Meanings go on expanding, and this is true of the Christmas stories themselves. In today's world with its appalling problems of hunger, homelessness and poverty, and as we think of the millions of refugees whose homes and livelihoods have been destroyed, and as we remember those in our own country who have lost their jobs and defaulted on their mortgages and who feel themselves to be unwanted, it is natural to see, in the story of Jesus born in a manger and driven into exile, a sign that God shares the lot of the outcasts.

I think it is highly unlikely that this is what the gospel writers actually had in mind. They were much more interested in the fulfilment of prophecy, hence the echoes of the Old Testament throughout the stories. For instance Isaiah had begun his prophecies: 'The ox knows its owner and the ass its master's crib [the word is the same as 'manger'], but Israel does not know, my people do not consider.' Israel had forgotten the one who feeds them. So the story of new life in Christ begins with a return to the place where God expects his people to be – at the master's crib. And Jesus wasn't born in an inn, because inns are for travellers, for people passing by, whereas this child had come to stay in the place where God sustains his people.

Matthew, who tells us about the exile in Egypt, again and again uses the imagery of Jesus as the new Moses. Just as Moses had been saved at the time of his birth when Pharaoh had ordered all the male Israelite children to be slaughtered, so Jesus was saved from the wrath of Herod. And just as the Israelites themselves were eventually brought out of exile in Egypt under the leadership of Moses, so Jesus himself, as the embodiment of the new Israel, comes out of Egypt too.

To say that this is the kind of meaning the gospel writers were trying to convey is not to deny that Jesus can also be seen as the friend of the homeless, the poor, and the refugees. But this is an expanded meaning, a meaning which comes out of later reflection on the Gospels, a meaning which nowadays may touch us more closely than the world of imagery in which the writers themselves moved.

The same is true, I suspect, of our present-day emphasis on the baby Jesus; on the innocence and purity and simplicity which Christmas heart-rendingly sets in contrast with the cynicism and world-weary sophistication of so much of modern life. We live in a 'nudge nudge wink wink' society. We are eager to cut people down to size. We lap up scandal. We are ready to believe the worst. Have you noticed how commentators on radio and television, even when describing something moderately successful, invariably slip in a final sentence to throw doubt on it and to suggest that there is worse to come?

Cynicism is the bitterest fruit of that critical spirit which in better times has done so much to lay the foundations of our Western civilization. Cynicism is criticism gone sour. And so for a brief moment we long for an image of innocence. We long to see God in the face of a child. And rightly so. St Paul saw with blinding clarity that God is known in the weak things of the world, in the despised and rejected, not in the powerful and the strong. But this truth was for him rooted in the cross of Christ, not in the baby Jesus of the nativity stories. Our modern emphasis, our necessary emphasis, on the innocence of a holy child, is an expanded meaning, just like the expanded meaning of that tiny door in Bethlehem.

This notion of expanded meaning can, I believe, bring us a bit closer to grasping the great mystery of the incarnation itself. We are not celebrating a fairy tale today. We are saying that those who first knew Jesus found the meaning of his life expanding and expanding until it filled their whole horizon. They piled image upon image to express their experience. And so discipleship turned into wonderment, and wonderment into worship, and worship eventually into the theology which speaks of God and man, the Word made flesh, the only-begotten Son of the Father.

And within Christian experience this process has continued. The life of Jesus is not a story which ended two thousand years ago, but, as the last verse of St John's Gospel reminds us, the book is still being written. In our bewildered, painful, often despairing world there is still the presence of one who comes, who calls, who gives life and light and healing, who is revealed to us in the simplicity of childhood and in the awful desolation of suffering. And as of old, those who respond to his call and allow him to expand their own horizons of meaning, discover in experience who he is. And with those who first saw his glory, we come to worship.

PART
2

Science, Faith and Ethics

5

The Bible and Scientific Discovery

Essay in Using the Bible Today, *edited by Dan Cohn-Sherbok,*
Bellew 1991

The Bible is pre-scientific. The same is true of the thinking of
many people today who, though living in a culture strongly
fashioned by the fruits of scientific discovery, remain largely
unaffected by its intellectual basis. Thus difficulties which
might have arisen from the impact of scientific ways of
thinking on the Bible are often not felt as acutely as perhaps
they should be. There is a widespread assumption that, give or
take a few much-discussed problems, the Bible can be read as if
it came out of the same kind of world as our own.

Others fall into the opposite error, and assume that a pre-
scientific book has nothing to teach the twentieth century. To
equate scientific knowledge with the totality of knowledge is
as foolish as imagining that the Bible has some kind of quasi-
scientific purpose.

There is an expectation in some quarters, for example, that
the Bible can somehow give direct answers to twentieth-
century questions, despite the fact that these questions could
not possibly have been in the minds of those who wrote it.
Psalm 139 was extensively used in recent debates on embryo
research. It was assumed almost without question by many
people that verses 13–16, which describe the secret fashioning

of a human being in the womb, could give authoritative guidance about precisely when, in the complex and gradual process of human generation, it is possible to identify human personhood. The psalm makes profound and important points about God's loving care for all human life from its beginning to its end, but it cannot adjudicate in scientific and philosophical disputes about the nature and stages of that beginning, because the questions which need to be answered could not even be formulated until a few decades ago.

This is not to say that the Bible cannot often deepen our insight into scientific issues. The example merely cautions against attempts to use it in a direct fashion as a source of scientific understanding. To read the Bible with integrity means coming to terms with the fact that in the last three hundred years the world has undergone a major intellectual revolution. Despite current criticisms of the Enlightenment and its aftermath, there is no going back on the main features of that revolution. Nor can the claim that the Bible offers an alternative world view to science, on science's own ground, be convincingly maintained.

One consequence of these changes has been a certain distancing between most people's experience of the natural world and perceptions of God's activity. Thus the description of a thunderstorm in Psalm 29 vividly portrays it in terms of God shouting through the trees, whirling the desert sands and inducing the cattle to calve. The fact that twentieth-century readers know a great deal more than the psalmist about weather patterns and electrical discharges need not diminish the feelings of awe which thunder and lightning can generate. Nor is it impossible to respond to them as images of God's glory and power. But it is more difficult nowadays than in biblical times to ascribe them to God's direct intervention unless, as happened with the lightning strike at York Minster, there is a prior wish to make theological capital out of an otherwise natural event. On average about a hundred churches in England are damaged by lightning every year.

It is more usual to speak of God as ultimately responsible for the majesty of a storm in the same sense in which he is ultimately responsible for everything, and to see him as ultimately revealed through such events in the same sense in which he can ultimately be revealed through other phenomena.

But the relationship thus described is a good deal more distant than that envisaged by the psalmist. Science has focused attention on immediate and intermediate causes, and it is preoccupation with such causes that chiefly distinguishes our own world from that of biblical times. In the biblical drama God is the main actor. In the context of scientific rationality he is more likely to be identified as the producer of the play, or its author or, more distantly still, as the owner of the theatre.

There is no easy way to overcome this sense of distance. It is partly, as I have hinted, a matter of expectations. To treat the Bible as a source of information on all sorts of subjects which lay outside the ken of its authors is to invite disappointment. To treat its contents as documents of their time which, within the particular constraints of their time, can reveal God's presence in history and in the world of nature, is to find it still speaking, albeit in a different mode. The God thus revealed may not be a God who directly causes thunderstorms, but he remains the God whose glory shines through such phenomena, and whose awesomeness is reflected in their power.

Creation

This contrast between direct and detailed intervention, and divine activity made effective through intermediate causes, comes to a sharp focus in different interpretations of the act or process of creation.

'By the Word of the Lord were the heavens made.' Psalm 33.6 echoes the theology of such passages as Isaiah 45.18 and the formal account of creation in Genesis 1. Creation is by God's direct command, by fiat. God speaks and it is done. All things come directly from God, and the implication is that most natural things are what they are because God designed them that way. Genesis 1 not only describes the ordered universe as expressing God's intention for his creation, but sets out the stages by which he actually brought it into being. Such was the view almost universally held by biblical interpreters until scientists began to disclose something of the size, age, complexity and interrelatedness of the natural world, and the causal connections within it.

An alternative account of creation, taking seriously the

story as told by scientists, sees the role of God as at one remove from this direct kind of interventionism. God works through natural laws. In the words of one theologian, 'He makes creation make itself'. The biblical story sets out the inner meaning of the scientific story by revealing the dependence of all existence on God, and the ultimate meaning of it as finding its fulfilment in God. But it does not provide detailed information about how and why things come to be. Answers to such questions have to be found by study of the things themselves, not by looking for short cuts in Scripture.

Thus crudely stated, the contrast can help to reinforce the point already made about the distancing between God and everyday experience of the world. Nevertheless it is only half the story. Biblical statements about creation did not arise out of philosophical reflection or from the kind of concerns which motivate scientists. The great passages in Isaiah 40–55 which historically mark the first clear and unequivocal statements about the oneness of God and his creative power, were written to a people in exile who needed to rediscover themselves as a nation, and to summon up the immense effort required to return and rebuild their country. They were reminded in glowing language of God's deliverance in the past and his supreme authority over world history in the present. And they were called to allow themselves to be recreated, to allow God to do 'a new thing' (43.19) with them. The concept of God as universal Creator, in other words, grew out of the lived experience of being rescued from exile.

Genesis 1 was almost certainly written at about the same time and represents essentially the same theology, developed and expanded and set in a different context, but rooted in the same lived experience. The God who separated light from darkness and ordered the world of nature, and showed man his role within it, is the same God who creates a nation out of runaway slaves from Egypt, and recreates it after its death in Babylon. And he is the same God whose Word is made flesh in Jesus Christ for the salvation, not just of a single people, but of the world.

Read against this human and historical background the Genesis creation narrative can speak just as directly of God as it did before Darwin wrote *The Origin of Species*. Perhaps even more directly, because it no longer has to do Darwin's work for him.

There is a further twist to the story in that the origin of modern science itself is nowadays increasingly seen to have depended on philosophical assumptions in medieval Europe derived from this very same biblical doctrine of creation. For science as we now know it, to be a worthwhile enterprise there has to be a prior belief that the universe is intelligible, but that its intelligibility is of a kind which cannot be deduced from first principles – in the way that Aristotle deduced that the orbits of the planets must be circular because this is the perfect shape in a perfect heaven. Without the belief that the world is intelligible there is no point in trying to understand otherwise puzzling phenomena. Without the recognition that deduction from first principles will not yield true knowledge of it there is no point in experimenting to find out how nature actually works. Only belief in an orderly creation made to be what it is by the sovereign will of God (and hence not deducible from anything prior to that) was able to provide for those first scientists the philosophical framework they needed. This is why the modern world was born in a Christian culture. It was the Bible's gift to science.

Miracles

Worries about the miraculous element in the Bible are not peculiar to a scientific age. Some alleged miracles have always caused difficulties, and one of the devices used by the earliest biblical interpreters was to allegorize stories which seemed too outrageous when taken literally. Another favourite device has been to put forward naturalistic explanations of events interpreted as miraculous at the time only because they then seemed inexplicable. Many healings, for instance, may not seem so surprising in the light of growing knowledge of the complex interactions between body and mind. Weathermen have been busy explaining the Israelites' crossing of the Red Sea. And there have been more tortuous attempts to come to terms with the miraculous, such as the various unconvincing explanations of the feeding of the 5000 based on the idea of the members of the crowd being induced to share their picnics.

Science may have changed some perceptions of what is or is not likely, but there is no clear scientific warrant for ruling out miracles as such. In fact the world as disclosed by science grows daily more strange and mysterious, and is far from the totally predictable, self-contained, machine-like entity which once had seemed to be implied by the early successes in physics. There was always an anomaly in the apparent existence of human creativity and free will in the midst of such a closed world, but nowadays physics itself has led the revolution towards an understanding of the world which is much more hospitable to novelty, freedom and indeterminacy. Most scientists very properly still retain a high degree of scepticism about the possibility of miracles because, as allegedly unique events, they cannot be brought within the scope of scientific investigation. But that is by no means the same as denying that they ever occur.

That said, the role of science in helping to distinguish between genuine mystery and absurdity remains vital. Twice in the Old Testament, for example, there are accounts of the sun being stopped, or reversed, in its tracks (2 Kings 20.11, Joshua 10.13). This would be a stupendous miracle by any standard, but less stupendous in a pre-Copernican universe. If the sun moves round the earth on a crystal sphere propelled by God, and if the inhabited earth itself is believed to be small and centred on Palestine, it is not totally unreasonable to suppose that God might for good reason temporarily stop his propulsion. But if stopping the sun means in effect stopping the rotation of the earth, with the result that everything on it would tend to fly off at huge velocity, and if Palestine is only one small corner of a large and populous world, the 'miraculous effort' involved in assuring Hezekiah that he was going to recover from his sickness, or in allowing Joshua time to smite a few more Amorites, would seem to be disproportionate. It is not enough to plead that with God all things are possible. Possible maybe, but not plausible. The stories either have to be dismissed, or interpreted some other way, if the concept of God they presuppose is not to be discredited. And that is so for theological, not scientific reasons, though science in this instance helps to sharpen the theological questions.

The stories are admittedly marginal to the main biblical themes. However, they provide a useful illustration of the notion of 'miraculous effort' which may possibly serve as a criterion in the interpretation of other miracle stories. 'Miraculous effort' is not a crude measure of the extra work God might be supposed to have done in performing a particular miracle, but of the appropriateness of the match between a striking event and the lessons to be learnt from it. A miracle has to be perceived as revelatory, as an event which discloses something of the power and presence of God. Its strangeness invites attention to what God is saying or doing through it. But if God does not seem to be saying very much it becomes a mere wonder, a source of amazement rather than faith. And if the message is trivial in comparison with the disruption of natural forces which might have been entailed, there is every reason for scepticism.

Jesus clearly rejected the description of himself as a wonder-worker, and this is why biblical scholars have generally looked with suspicion at alleged miracles, like the coin in the fish's mouth (Matthew 17.27), which seem to fall into the category of wonders, and are probably best interpreted as parables or folk tales. Genuine miracles, by contrast, are best interpreted as signs, and what they signify is more important than the oddity of their occurrence. If changes in understanding make them seem less odd, or throw doubt on the way the story is told, this may not diminish their value as signs whose meaning lies in what they tell us of God. In St John's Gospel the theological superstructure built around the seven great signs which form the core of the Gospel far outweighs the 'miraculous effort' in the signs themselves.

This is even more true in the case of the resurrection. As an event it seems inexplicable by any standards, and attempts to explain it in psychological and quasi-physical terms seem to evacuate it of its primary significance, that death itself has in some way been robbed of its finality. It is at this point supremely that faith has to make its claims in the face of normal scientific expectations. But it is at this point also that the 'miraculous effort' entailed entirely matches the enormous implications. No miracle could be more appropriate, nor more fully vindicated in the subsequent experience of believers.

Science as an aid to biblical study

Though the Bible is not a source of scientific understanding, it records events which may or may not be illuminated, or even directly verified, by scientific study. High hopes have at times been vested in archaeology, but attempts to match archaeological discoveries with particular biblical events have proved frustratingly inconclusive. There is still no agreement, for instance, about the chronology of the exodus. Clear signs of cultural change in ancient village sites can provide evidence of migrations and conquests. But the pattern which has emerged over many years of archaeological investigation in Palestine is a great deal more complex than the Old Testament version of events. The study of the site of Jericho, for instance, has led to intense debates over many years, some striking claims and counter-claims, and no agreement.

Some of the most interesting discoveries have been on the sites of former royal palaces. Solomon's wealth and reputation as a builder can in part be documented, and much attention was devoted some years ago to the excavation of the so-called royal stables at Megiddo. It now appears that these were probably not stables after all, nor were they built by Solomon, and that a later dynasty may actually have exceeded him in material power. Such reversals of opinion are typical of the uncertainties inherent in this kind of study.

Archaeology's main value in biblical interpretation has been to illuminate the culture of biblical times by the study of places and artefacts, and in this role it can help to verify how frequently the biblical narratives ring true. Other sciences can sometimes perform a similar function, though not with much conviction. Medical insights in Luke and Acts have been much discussed, and have persuaded some people of Luke's authorship, while failing to convince others. The famous description of the plague in 1 Samuel 5.6—6.6 with its reference to rats and death-dealing tumours suggests an early and accurate insight into the relationship between them. Some of the plagues of Egypt in Exodus 7—10 form a more or less credible sequence on the assumption that they were triggered off by a red muddy silt in the River Nile ('blood'), though the fact that the reddening of the Nile tended to be a fairly frequent occurrence obviously weakens the case for regarding the plagues as especially disastrous.

Such meagre gleanings from science in aid of biblical interpretation stand in sharp contrast to the claims made by much contemporary popular fundamentalist literature. This abounds with misconceived efforts to 'prove' the flood by the study of sediments, to 'discover' Noah's ark still mysteriously lodged on Mount Ararat, and to vindicate the scientific accuracy of incidental statements in Scripture as evidence of its verbal inspiration. Such efforts are usually tendentious and futile, and distract attention from the character of revelation to which the central tenets of the Christian faith bear witness.

God, so Christians claim, was incarnate in a human life at a particular place and time, and in being so subjected himself to the limitations of that place and time. In his incarnate life he had no privileged access to knowledge which belongs to the twentieth century, nor did those who in earlier ages wrote out of the lived experience of God's presence among them. The cultural distancing described at the beginning of this chapter means that this age, like other ages before it, has to learn how to read the story of God's dealings with his world in the light of its own best knowledge. It also has to let the story challenge this knowledge and its own presuppositions, and to learn how to integrate both perspectives through reflection (especially on its own past), through worship, and through actually living the Christian life. Signs embedded in the story which enable us to relate it to discoveries in our own era, can help to increase confidence in it. But science itself can neither establish nor disprove its tremendous message.

6

Response to Richard Dawkins

Article published in The Independent *shortly after the debate on science and religion at the Edinburgh Science Festival, May 1992*

In the Edinburgh Science Festival's debate on science and religion between Richard Dawkins and myself, the comment from the floor which came nearest the heart of things was that it ought really to have been about philosophy. When two ways of thinking appear to be at such odds with each other, the only sensible approach is to try to identify the second-order questions which underlie the differences, questions about the assumptions and aims of the two activities.

In my own opening contribution to the debate this is what I had tried to do. Put very crudely, science is the exploration of patterns of relationship between phenomena. Religion is about the reality which underlies all phenomena, and the attempt to discern its meaning for human life. Such a neat and abstract distinction, however, does not in practice match the actual complexities of life. I therefore tried to demonstrate something of the historically shifting relationship between the two, from the early dependence of science on its theological background, through the centuries of its struggle for autonomy, to our own century with its scientific revolutions, which have opened the way to a new partnership in which both are acknowledged as representing important, though different, aspects of human experience.

Richard Dawkins would have none of this. His crude caricature of believers as 'know-nothings', 'know-alls', and 'no-contests' was a contemptuous dismissal of the whole of this history. It is true that there are some believers who cling unreasonably to faith as if it were an alternative to science. It is also true that there are others who evacuate the contents of faith to the point at which it no longer makes any claims about the nature of reality. But it is emphatically not true to say that, by defining science and religion as being about different aspects of reality, one is playing some kind of dishonest game in which the distinction between fact and fiction is blurred.

Most of the centuries-long discussion about science and religion has taken place in this middle ground where the complex relationship between facts and their interpretation still keeps philosophers busy. Only the most unphilosophically minded scientists now suppose that pure and simple facts can be known to us outside a framework of interpretation, which is itself the product of a long history. And it would be a foolish theologian who failed to recognize that theological claims are likewise culturally conditioned. Simple oppositions of the kind Richard Dawkins delights in are good material for repartee, but brush all such considerations aside.

Take his comments on 'the big bang of modern cosmology' and 'the myth of Genesis'. 'There is only an utterly trivial resemblance between the sophisticated, esoteric conceptions of modern physics, and the creation myths of the Babylonians and the Jews that we have inherited.' In a superficial sense that is true, as is his earlier remark that the highly attenuated concept of God put forward by some physicists 'bears absolutely no resemblance to the God of the Bible'.

But once we take the trouble to look beneath the surface and ask how these two accounts have historically influenced one another, a much more complex story emerges. Many of the early cosmologists appealed to the Bible as the source of their belief that there was an intelligible order to be found in the universe. Likewise theologians, forced to recognize that Genesis could not be interpreted as if it were a scientific account, began to see that its origins lay, not in some kind of quasi-scientific speculation, but in historical experience.

The biblical story of creation emerged from a people in exile, wondering whether their trust in God had been misplaced, and whether this God to whom they had given their allegiance was powerful enough to turn the course of history once again in their favour. The great Hebrew prophets answered emphatically that he was. They asserted confidently that the God of their people was the only God, the one who brought order out of chaos, the Creator, and the saviour of those who trusted in him. Their achievement was to see meaning in an experience which otherwise could have been interpreted as sheer meaningless tragedy. Those who believed the promise found it was true, and Judaism and Christianity exist today because some people had the courage to act on that faith. This was the historical experience, out of which the Genesis narrative came to be written, and in this light it can be understood as a statement about God as the one in whom the meaning and order of the created world resides.

What kind of correlation might we expect to find with twentieth-century physics? Clearly it would be nonsensical to look for correlations with actual physical or cosmological theories, and to that extent whether there was a big bang or whether there will eventually be a big crunch makes no difference to theology. However, theologians may rightly see significance in the fact that the latest big bang discoveries help to confirm what has been believed for a long time, namely that the universe is an ordered and intelligible whole. That insight is the foundation on which the whole structure of science has been built. Its vindication, in the actual discernment of intelligibility, coupled with the fact that it is possible to push our understanding of cosmology back to unimaginable beginnings, tells us something rather surprising, not only about the universe, but also about ourselves and our own mental processes. And it is not trivial. Nor is it trivial to wonder at the fact that anything exists at all. Nor is it trivial to wonder whether the way in which nuclear physics keeps pointing us back to an awareness of ourselves as observers, tells us something about the blurred boundaries between objective and subjective experience. The sense of wonder which such discoveries can induce at least bears some resemblance to the awe felt by those early Israelites who dared to believe that their world was not meaningless.

It is true that the God of the physicists and the God of the

Bible may seem to belong to two different worlds of thought. I have sketched out one link between them. The fact that other links have been made in other ways in other historical periods only serves to show that questions about meaning thrown up by the study of the natural world do not easily go away.

Some people can and do shut their minds against religious reality. Religions have always been fair game for debunkers, because the search for meaning is a subtle and delicate enterprise which needs a certain sympathy and sensitivity if it is to succeed. Yet they remain astonishingly persistent, so persistent in fact that it is hard not to conclude that, despite the multifarious history of religions, the religious quest itself is testimony to some basic kind of reality.

There is a certain irony in some words written by William James at the turn of the century: 'Every sort of energy and endurance, of courage and capacity for handling life's evils, is set free in those who have religious faith. For this reason the strenuous type of character will on the battlefield of human history always outwear the easy-going type, and religion will drive irreligion to the wall.' The implication seems to be that in a Darwinian world the religious are best fitted to survive. In a desperate attempt to explain this capacity for survival, Dr Dawkins has postulated the equivalent of a computer virus in human brains as responsible for a massive religious infection. With that kind of argument it is possible to explain anything.

The real offence of religion in the eyes of such critics lies, I suspect, in its appeal to realms of experience outside scientific competence. For Dawkins, it would seem the only kind of knowledge worth having is scientific knowledge. In this he reveals himself as an old-fashioned positivist, as are many practising scientists who have been so impressed by the enormous success of their subject in gathering and ordering one kind of knowledge, that it has become for them the only standard for all knowledge and all truth. Dawkins has done excellent work in evolutionary theory by demonstrating how complexity can arise out of simplicity. But he has moved from science to scientism in making this the key to his universe, even to the point of ridiculing God for not conforming to his pattern.

The temptation to stretch science beyond its limits is particularly strong in the case of evolutionary theory because the key concepts at the heart of it are so simple and adaptable. Ideas of continuity and change, adaptation and competition seem infinitely extensible. But it is precisely because of this that care needs to be exercised in applying biological criteria and insights to matters which lie outside the realm of biology. The frightful things done in the name of Social Darwinism should be sufficient warning.

The obvious fallacy in a positivist approach to science is that if you search the universe for certain kinds of connections, those and those only are what you will find. Everything else slips through the net. God does not appear in the scientific account of things because both the objectives and methods of science are deliberately oblivious of anything which might be a pointer to God, any hint of purpose or intention or feeling or value. This is not a criticism of science. It is simply a description of what science is, and the key to what makes it so successful in studying those aspects of reality in which purpose, feeling, value and so forth are not of prime importance.

Religious experience, on the other hand, points to truths which elude this kind of treatment. Our knowledge of people, for instance, not as objects to be analysed, but as persons to be encountered, is just as real as our knowledge of stars or genes – in fact more so because it is more direct and involves more of our capacities. Historical knowledge, too, is not reducible to science, and has strong links with religion. It sharpens awareness of the fact that all knowledge belongs within a historical context, even scientific knowledge, and all entails historically conditioned interpretation. Then there is the kind of truth which can only be conveyed in stories. Biblical interpretation has to reckon with the many layers of meaning which have accumulated through a long historical process of testing and winnowing claims about God in actual life.

Teasing out the relationship between these different kinds of knowledge, and exposing the fatal consequences of a lop-sided concentration on only one kind, is a job for philosophy. I am aware, of course, that such philosophical reflection does not of itself make the task of defending religious faith any easier. But at least it could have rescued the Edinburgh debate from the superficial badinage which prevented any serious attempt at wrestling with the real problems. And it might have shown up more clearly the blinkering effect of an exclusive concentration on science, which in the hands of some of its single-minded practitioners can develop its own quasi-religious mythology. Dr Dawkins's name will, I suppose, be forever associated with 'The Selfish Gene' – a more blatant piece of anthropomorphism than any found within Christian theology.

7

The Human Fertilization and Embryology Bill

Lecture delivered at King's College, London, 19 February 1990

The clauses concerning embryo research in this Bill are controversial, and will go on being controversial, despite the large Parliamentary majorities in favour of allowing some research under strictly controlled conditions. Sharp disagreements of this kind usually reflect different ethical presuppositions. It may be useful, therefore, to set out in a very simple form the different types of question which provide the criteria for such decisions, and which may carry different weight in different ethical traditions. Broadly speaking, there are four types of question: those to do with principles, those to do with consequences, those to do with precedents and those to do with motives.

All are important in the attempt to find a broad ethical consensus on which to base legislation. To analyse a problem under these four headings does not necessarily make it any easier to agree. Discussions on contentious issues are rarely conclusive. But to understand why there are disagreements can take some of the sharpness out of debate, and help to remove misunderstandings. I intend to look at each area of questioning in turn, taking them in reverse order.

1. Motives

Good motives do not excuse actions which are wrong on other grounds. Equally, bad motives do not necessarily invalidate good actions, despite T. S. Eliot's strictures against doing 'the right thing for the wrong reason'. Personal motives may well have major moral significance in the assessment of individual actions, but in the realm of public policy, motives are frequently mixed and extremely difficult to assess. Where there is evidence to suspect bad motives, however, these can arouse justifiable suspicion about the ethical validity of a particular choice.

There are good motives for wanting to undertake embryo research, of which the most obvious is the desire to improve therapy and to enlarge the area of therapeutically useful knowledge. There are also good reasons for wanting to ban research, of which the most obvious is the desire to protect and value human life in all its forms, and at all stages of development. Researchers might claim that they too share this motive, though they work out its implications in a different way, just as the opponents of research would claim that they too are concerned with therapy, though not at the cost of what they see as human lives.

It is in the suspicions about bad motives that the discussion in this area of questioning becomes more acrimonious. Researchers, for instance, may suspect that opposition to their work is all part of an anti-science campaign, and fear that a total ban on research in a potentially fruitful field might deliver a body blow to scientific confidence. Anti-researchers retaliate by drawing parallels with Nazi experiments on human beings; and it is noteworthy that in the House of Lords debate on the second reading of the Bill, the most emotional speech, and the one which received the attention in the press, drew precisely this parallel. The thin end of the wedge argument is also widely canvassed, and it has been strongly argued that the fourteen day limit for research will be quickly eroded, and that the researchers see this as a bridgehead rather than as a goal.

Accusations about hidden intentions have been most

vociferous among the anti-researchers, and the following quotation from an SPUC leaflet is not untypical: 'Using women's bodies as laboratories, and embryos as guinea pigs, will benefit principally the multi-national drug companies and the population controllers.' It would be difficult to pack more loaded words into a single sentence, except perhaps in the final exhortation which decorated this particular leaflet, 'Stop human vivisection now.'

Recognition of honourable motives on both sides can help civilized debate. Unfortunately, though, honourable motives are not enough, nor is it possible to rely on them in practice as the sole safeguard against abuse, despite the fact that voluntary controls on embryo research in this country have hitherto worked reasonably well. A legislative framework is needed, and becomes all the more necessary, as research passes out of the hands of the pioneers into a more commercial context.

2. Precedents

Much decision-making begins with the questions, What did we do last time? and, Are there any parallels? In the field of embryo research there are no strong precedents. Abortion is perhaps the closest, because attitudes towards abortion expose beliefs about the moral status of the embryo and foetus. There is a long Christian tradition in which abortion has been condemned at any and every stage of development, but there has also been a recognition that its degree of seriousness as an offence increases as the foetus grows older. There has been, in other words, an implicit acknowledgement that the moral significance of the foetus is not identical at all stages, though there are some who would fiercely contest this point of view.

Although ethical thinking about abortion can give clues, therefore, as to how an embryo or a conceptus ought to be treated, the moral dilemma posed by research is significantly different. Abortion is essentially about a conflict of evils, and the choices are centred on a particular mother and child, either or both of whom stand to gain or lose. The dilemma posed by research concerns the use of a conceptus, which can only be destroyed in the process, for the future benefit of others. There is a conflict of evils, but it does not focus on particular individuals who face an immediate problem. The existence of such conflict cannot, therefore, be as easily used to justify an act of destruction in the case of research as in the case of abortion, and it is best therefore not to treat one as a precedent for the other.

There are more general precedents which might offer guidance, notably the history of the acceptance of many medical techniques which were once regarded as morally dubious. Transplant surgery, for instance, was once felt to violate the sense of human dignity and integrity just as, in an earlier generation, vaccination was condemned as entailing an 'animalization' of human beings. Similar feelings surfaced in the more recent proposal to use pigs' hearts in human transplants. On the whole, the experience has been that techniques once regarded as shocking cease to shock in a comparatively short space of time. This may be through a blunting of moral sensibilities. Equally, it may be a belated recognition that the shock was unnecessary, and that human dignity and integrity survive these apparent assaults.

However, the changes in feeling are not all in one direction. Greater sensitivities about animal experiments and growing worries about abortion may be the tip of a large iceberg. Many people are expressing fears about an increasingly reductionist view of human life. There are fears about opening the door to wider eugenic programmes. There are fears about commercial pressures once they gain a hold in what is a potentially lucrative field. Indeed, in the United States interest is already being expressed by some large companies in the possibilities of drug testing on spare embryos.

History shows that the boundaries of the acceptable are by no means fixed, and do not always move in a more liberal direction. The present Bill would limit some activities which are at present uncontrolled by law, and give legal recognition to others, for example the donation of gametes, which at present are not protected by law. It is as well to recognize slippery slopes in all directions.

The appeal to Christian tradition as a guide in these matters can draw on a strong and consistent desire to protect human life in all its forms, with a special emphasis on its weakest and most vulnerable forms. The element of uncertainty in the tradition, and the potential for disagreement, lie in the realm of definitions. Advances in embryology have provided some Christians with support for their claim that human life begins at an identifiable moment, namely fertilization. This claim is put forward on the basis of Scripture and an unbroken historical tradition, despite the fact that human fertilization was described for the first time only in 1875. Other Christians have questioned whether this story of human origins and this definition of human life are as clear as they seem, and stress instead the emergence of a single identifiable embryo as an episode in a complex story. I shall return to this disagreement later. The point I wish to make now is that there is no particular reason based explicitly in Christian tradition for deciding in favour of one side or the other.

Direct appeals to such scriptural texts as Psalm 139 and Jeremiah 1.5 do not carry conviction, even if it were reasonable to suppose that the Scriptures are intended to give us detailed knowledge about the processes of human formation. The obvious meaning of such texts is that God has foreknowledge of us, and there is no time at which we fall outside his loving purposes. It is illegitimate to look in them for a definition of when this process begins. The appeal made by some Christians to the story of the Annunciation to Mary, and the virginal conception of Jesus, are equally dubious grounds for beliefs about embryology. Christians who assert in faith that these things happened are fortunately not required to say precisely how or when they happened, whereas it is precisely the how and when questions that are relevant to the moral issues under discussion.

To dismiss these specific Christian contributions to the debate is not to deny that there are serious questions to be considered about God's intentions in calling things to be. Can, or should, all potentials for life be realized? Or is the universe of a kind in which some frustration of potentials is inevitable? Lurking behind these questions, framed as they are in theological terms, are huge biologically-inspired questions about the significance of the fecundity of biological processes, and the corresponding problems of waste and destruction. It may be that God's intentions can only be seen with hindsight in the fulfilled potentiality of his creatures, rather than in the enormous quantity of unfulfilment which undergirds them.

3. Consequences

The assessment of the likely consequences of actions and policies is the most commonly cited basis for decision-making in the public sphere. Stated thus crudely, however, it does not take us very far. Every action may have endless consequences, and those consequences themselves need to be ethically evaluated. Some distinction needs to be made between relevant and irrelevant consequences, and this too may entail ethical judgement.

There are useful distinctions between immediate and long-term consequences, and individual and social consequences. On the whole, long-term consequences and social ones are harder to predict than immediate and individual ones, and therefore tend to weigh less heavily in the decision-making process. Medicine has a strong bias towards immediate and individual consequences. Doctors tend to focus their concern on the patient and the illness immediately in front of them. Research and preventative medicine take the long-term perspective, but still have a bias towards the needs of individuals. The way in which individuals are influenced by their social context, and the ways in which this can be adversely affected by short-term decisions, are often important factors in a religiously based ethic, but can seem too nebulous to those who have immediate decisions to make.

Within the embryo debate, attempts have been made to justify very limited forms of research on a conceptus or embryo which is itself likely to benefit directly from the research being done on it. In practice the opportunities afforded for this kind of research are so limited as to be valueless. Furthermore, it suffers from the grave moral objection that the risks entailed in it are risks to an actual mother and child, risks entailed at the leading edge of research, and that cannot be assessed for safety in the absence of the less direct kind of research provided for in the Bill.

The main difficulty in predicting the long-term social consequences of disallowing research on embryos is that nobody can tell what research might achieve until it has actually been done. Given the fact that *in vitro* fertilization at present has a low success rate, it seems fairly safe to assume that, in the absence of further research, this will not be greatly improved; there would thus be a serious question mark over the ethical propriety of continuing to use such an imperfect technique. It also seems reasonable to assume that to forbid research in a particular area for reasons which were not seen by the researchers themselves to have ethical validity, might further widen the gulf between scientists and the rest of the community at a time when scientists themselves are already feeling undervalued.

The main long-term social consequence of allowing research might be a devaluation of human life, a further step in the long process of treating human beings as objects. On the other hand, if the aims of research are clearly therapeutic, and if the procedures clearly result in the birth of healthy babies to couples who have long been wanting them, then it would be argued that the social consequences of such research might be to increase the valuation of human life, by virtue of the heroic measures undertaken to produce it.

Similarly, it can be argued on the one hand that genetic selection at the pre-implantation stage devalues the lives of the disabled. But it can also be claimed that such selection might provide enormous help and encouragement to those who know they are the carriers of genetic defects, by greatly increasing their chances of bearing a normal child.

These arguments are tenuous. Most of them depend upon the way in which perceptions change as practices change. Furthermore, the setting up of legislative safeguards can in itself have a major influence on public attitudes. Effective control mechanisms can, in this respect, be as significant as outright prohibition; it does not follow, therefore, that long-term social considerations about human devaluation require the latter. As regards the more immediate consequences of research, the onus is on the researchers to demonstrate that their work has major therapeutic possibilities, and on the legislators to demonstrate the exceptional nature of the permission given to work in such a sensitive area.

4. Principles

Despite the fact that most decisions in the public sphere rest on an assessment of likely consequences, however difficult this might prove to be, the appeal to principles can, and in some circumstances must, have decisive weight. In the field of secular ethics Kant, as it were, acts as a corrective to Mill. In the Christian context, the belief that there are moral absolutes outweighs any argument from expediency.

The question is, therefore, whether embryo research violates a principle of such importance that all other consider-ations are irrelevant. Does research break the principle of respect for human life in such a way as to settle the matter? Or are the uncertainties in the application of this principle to the human conceptus so great as to open up the argument to all the other considerations which have so far been adduced? In what sense, in other words, can the conceptus be said to deserve the respect and protection given to a human being?

There need be no dispute over the fact that such a conceptus is human in a descriptive sense. It needs to be noted, however, that the word 'human' is used both descriptively and evalu-atively, and the former need not always entail the latter. It is an open question as to when something described as 'human' needs to carry the full moral connotations of the word.

It is also clear that a conceptus forms part of a continuous history in which fertilization is a decisive, but not the only decisive, event. Much of the technical argument about embryo research has focused on the earliest period of development at which genetic identity is fixed, but the cellular identity of the developing organism is not. In the stage of undifferentiated growth following fertilization, any one of the large number of cells in the conceptus may develop into the embryo and, in some cases, into more than one embryos. To say that fertilization is the beginning of a human life, therefore, as if from that moment human identity were fixed, is to oversimplify a confused and complex process.

The argument that, despite the fluidity of personal identity at this earliest stage, it is nevertheless reasonable to recognize and respect the potential of the developing organism, is frequently stated and has considerable strength. Yet there is something logically strange about giving high valuation to potential, when there is as yet no clearly definable entity which possesses that potential, and before the conditions, notably implantation, have begun to be fulfilled through which alone that potential can be realized.

From a biological perspective, the significance of genetic union is that it provides a new source of information and sets in motion a process through which a new being, and ultimately a new person, is formed. This process is not simply an unfolding of what is already there, but is an actual process of creation through interactions both inside and outside the developing organism. From this perspective it makes little sense to say that at one moment there is a human being, whereas a few moments previously there was not. Biological processes are in general not amenable to such sharp distinctions, and therefore fit uncomfortably into legal definitions. If it is asked from a legal point of view whether a conceptus is a thing or a person, the only sensible answer is neither. It is an organism on the way to becoming a person. Given the right conditions its personhood will develop with the development of certain attributes, and the most basic and rudimentary of these is cellular identity which becomes fixed at around the time of the formation of the primitive streak.

Arguments from principle based on the nature of the conceptus are thus not as clear and straightforward as reliance on them to provide moral absolutes might suggest. This uncertainty corresponds to ordinary moral perceptions as evidenced, for example, in attitudes towards miscarriages. A miscarriage may be seen as a tragic event, and I would not wish in any way to underplay the sense of loss which might be felt after even a very early miscarriage. It is noticeable, however, that the fruits of the miscarriage are not generally treated with the respect due to a human life. The need for some kind of funeral service for still-born babies is achieving wider and wider recognition, but miscarriages are usually flushed away down the drain without much sense that this is inappropriate or disrespectful. As in the case of abortion, there seems to be a sliding scale on which the intrinsic value of the growing foetus is acknowledged as the relationship between mother and unborn child develops, and there seems to be something curiously artificial about acknowledging full human value in a conceptus which has not even been implanted.

Should not its unique, genetic constitution, however, invite respect? Here again, it is important to distinguish between such a unique genetic constitution and personal identity. Identical twins have the same genetic constitution, but are different people. Genetic uniqueness is certainly significant in retrospect. Each of us is what we are by reason of a chance configuration of genes among billions and billions of possibilities. It does not follow, however, that every one of those possibilities has to be treated as potentially of infinite value before any unique attributes of an individual have actually begun to develop. Here, as earlier, arguments from potential seem to me to try to prove too much. Biological processes entail selection from among vast stores of potential, and it is only in the processes following this selection that distinctive value begins to emerge.

A zygote formed *in vitro*, and isolated for purposes of research outside the context of a personal life history and set of personal relationships, belongs within a context where only very limited potential will or can be fulfilled. Its intrinsic value is not that of a person, though neither is it negligible. Restrictive legislation concerning its treatment can help to strengthen our perceptions of it as belonging within the total mystery of human life, while not giving it so much moral significance as to override all other considerations about what may be done with it.

There is no certainty about moral decision-making in this complex area. We are right to be cautious. We are right also to remember that embryo research has been in progress for about twenty years without obvious abuse and, for the first time, we are imposing legal restrictions on it. I am not persuaded that the case against research is so strong as to require absolute prohibition, and although I believe that some of the moral argument in the Warnock Report side-stepped the major issues, the actual proposals in the Report in my judgement got the balance about right.

Note

This essay is also published in *Challenges in Medical Care*, edited by A. Grubb, John Wiley 1992.

8

The Perils of Trying to Know Too Much

Lecture delivered at the Second National Conference on Genetics, Religion and Ethics, Houston, Texas, 13 March 1992

My title may justifiably cause some alarm. In scientific circles the idea that it is possible to know too much, or worse, the prospect that there might be some areas of forbidden knowledge, are major heresies. Modern science takes its title deeds from Francis Bacon: 'The end of our foundation is the knowledge of causes and secret motions of things, to the effecting of all things possible.' To suggest otherwise would be to cut at the root of that freedom, curiosity, boldness and disinterested love of truth, which, ideally at least, has been the driving force of scientific endeavour.

Yet clearly this cannot be the whole story. Given powers which Bacon in his wildest dreams could not have imagined, most of us are less enthusiastic than he was about 'effecting all things possible'. The urgent question is not, What *can* we do? but, What *should* we do? Less compelling nowadays, too, is the assertion that knowledge is some kind of absolute value whose claims outweigh all other claims. Jacques Monod's attempt to give it this status in the well-known conclusion to his book *Chance and Necessity*, simply revealed the arbitrary nature of his basic commitment, as he himself had the honesty to admit. To pursue knowledge at any price and whatever the consequences may seem heroic. But it is a goal which ignores and may threaten too much else that is human. In any event it overlooks the complexities in the idea of knowledge itself. Here again I suggest the question should be, not, What can we *know*? but, What is *worth* knowing? and what does it *mean* to know it?

I had my first lesson along these lines as a young research student when I read, in the obituary of a physiologist I admired, that he had spent his life reducing the quantity of literature on colour vision. It was a nice way of highlighting the distinction between information and knowledge, between quantity and quality. And that is perhaps the most obvious and elementary peril in trying to know too much, that of burdening ourselves with information that cannot actually be used, and that only serves to complicate our choices.

My second lesson followed immediately from this in my own work on the study of sensation. It is well known now, but was not at all obvious then, that the sensory information reaching our brains is drastically filtered at several stages on the way, and sometimes suppressed entirely. There is not a simple one-to-one connection between stimulus, transmission and sensation, and if there were we would be overloaded with information to the point of paralysis. I suppose the most striking example of the suppression of sensory information has been in the study of war wounds, when over and over again those who have suffered the most frightful injuries have actually felt nothing. In the study of sensation, inhibition is as important as excitation. To make the point in general terms, there are differences between information, interpreted information and appropriate information, and even at a simple physical level sensory systems are adapted to distinguish between them.

All this may seem distant from the main theme of our conference, but I am concerned to make the point that even in simple scientific contexts the idea of 'knowledge' is not entirely straightforward, and that the complexities increase enormously when we set out to know the intimate basis of human life. I am intrigued, for instance, that in the early days of the Human Genome Project this was described again and again as 'the grail of human genetics'. Borne up by such rhetoric, it became the unstoppable quest, the ultimate search for the essence of humanity, the blueprint for understanding human biology. No doubt a certain amount of hype was necessary to persuade the politicians to fund it. But there is a quasi-mystical element in the way it was presented which made the word 'grail' strangely appropriate. The grail of medieval legend was indeed symbolic of the quest for the secret of life. It was also about magical powers. It has strong moral and religious overtones. But above all the grail was systematically elusive; it was the quest for it which became significant rather than the hope of finding it. I wonder how far search for the grail of human genetics will in time be seen to share these same characteristics – both good and bad.

Already there have been changes. The original aim, as I understand it, was to attack the problem on three levels. First the genetic map, itself a huge task, but closely related to identifiable human characteristics. Secondly the physical map, concerned much more directly with the positioning of genes on the DNA. Thirdly, the goal of the whole process, the sequence itself, the map depicting all three billion positions of its nucleotides. It was this third goal that initially captured popular imagination, but that now seems to be receding in significance in favour of more immediate and practically useful goals. In my own country, for instance, genome research has always been disease-led. This is partly because there is not much money for it, but also partly because it seems much more sensible to tackle problems which actually need to be solved, than to set off on a great quest for ultimate secrets when it is not clear that these are going to be worth having.

I am not technically equipped to discuss the pros and cons of complete sequencing. I can see the value of building up a vast data base as a kind of reference map, despite the frequent claim that only about three per cent of it will convey useful genetic information. But, against that, I can also see that the larger the data base the more difficult it is to devise ways of handling it, especially when, as now seems likely, parts of the work are going to be contracted out to commercial interests. I can see the challenge of climbing the equivalent of a biological Mount Everest 'because it is there'. But then I am also conscious that the best science has about it a certain elegance and economy, which the mind-blowing tedium of large-scale sequencing at present seems to lack. I can see the point of postponing much of the sequencing work until the technology is available for it to be automated. But if in the meantime attention is focused on those parts of it which are medically and biologically most important, I wonder how much will be lost if the full work is never done. That ninety-seven per cent of the DNA sequence now labelled 'junk' worries me. Does the fact that no function has been found for it mean that it has no function? And if so, what sort of evolutionary explanation might there be for such a high level of redundancy?

I believe it is healthy that the aims of the exercise should change as it progesses, not least so as to keep in view those human questions about its purpose, which are apt to drop out of sight when a scientific project begins to turn into a technological race. The accumulation of massive amounts of information is not knowledge, though it may provide a basis for knowledge. Knowledge is more than an abstract pattern in the mind or in the computer. It is an understanding of what to do with such patterns, how to use them. It is a claim to be able to take responsible decisions about some more or less reliable bit of the natural world. And where that knowledge relates to human beings, it is important that its connections with other aspects of human life are not broken or ignored.

The specialization within our academic world carries the penalty that disconnection happens all too easily. I like the cartoon of the astronomer's wife showing a visitor into his observatory. He sits there, his eye glued to a huge telescope, while his wife remarks, 'My husband lives in a little world of his own'. One could say the same of the human genome. In one sense the study of it opens the door to a vast world, a panorama embracing all living things. But on its own it is merely a little world of chemical patterns, available for selective inspection through a computerized data bank.

The point I am making applies to specialized knowledge in general. It is always part of a larger human-based understanding and set of purposes. But genetic knowledge has its own additional and peculiar problems in that the significance to be ascribed to it in the life of the complete organism is seldom totally clear. Where there is a one-to-one relationship between some identifiable genetic characteristic and some specific human trait or disease, then obviously that genetic information can be profoundly significant for that human life. But, as we know, most relationships are not of that kind. The combined effects of multiple genes in both normal and abnormal development rapidly blur the ability to trace exact connections. Even more important is the fact that genes are not simply creating structures, but controlling processes. The history of an organism, therefore, both in terms of the interactions between its parts and in terms of its interactions with its environment, is an irreducible factor in its having become what it is. There are historical connections to be traced, which cannot merely be subsumed into descriptions of chemical and physical causation, any more than the story of evolution can be reduced to such terms. And what is true of organisms in general is uniquely true of human beings.

Schizophrenia provides an obvious example. Almost certainly it depends on a genetic predisposition. Equally certainly, not all those predisposed develop into full-blown schizophrenics. There is strong evidence to suggest that stress of various kinds plays its part in the actual onset of the illness. There are also family considerations which seem to have an effect on the course of the illness. Some recent studies indicate that the acceptance or non-acceptance of schizophrenic behaviour within a family can be linked quite closely to recovery and recurrence. Here, then, is a subtle and complex human scenario, paralleled in countless other examples of normal and abnormal development. We learn from them that it is not just that the interaction between such varied factors is intricate and largely unpredictable, but that it is an interaction in which personal history and social relationships play an indispensable part.

What therefore does our genetic knowledge give us? Merely one factor in a long and tangled story. In some instances it may be the decisive factor. Central to the work done hitherto is the list of diseases in which genetic abnormalities seem to be life-determining. Even so, it is quite a short list. As it is extended to include a wider range of diseases, and still further to include normal human traits and characteristics, the lines of communication between genetic chemistry and human consequences seem increasingly tenuous. At every stage there are interpretations, interactions, and historical processes, so much so that the idea of drawing a clear dividing line between heredity and environment seems not just increasingly unreal, but increasingly irrelevant. Our knowledge of the basic chemistry of life undoubtedly tells us something. In assessing its significance, however, we need to be aware also of what we do not know, and in the nature of things cannot know. High-sounding language about 'the essence of humanity' confuses the building blocks with the finished product. The fact that we share ninety-eight per cent of our genes with chimpanzees does not mean that there is only a two per cent difference between being chimpanzee and being human – for most of us, at any rate.

In the study of human life the confusion between building blocks and finished product is particularly disastrous. One of the most striking characteristics of human life, as actually lived and experienced, is its open-endedness. To be human is to be unfinished and free. This is a theme well explored in Christian theology. 'It does not yet appear what we shall be, but we know that when he appears we shall be like him for we shall see him as he is' (1 John 3.2). St John's whole epistle is a profound exploration of the intimate relation between human life and God's life, of the idea that human beings only find fulfilment and completeness in loving and being loved, and that overarching our human loving is the infinite love of God. We cannot know what we are in any final sense until at the end we meet that love face to face.

That is one theological way of expressing our sense of incompleteness as human beings. St Paul put it another way. Our interdependence is spelt out in the imagery of building up the Body of Christ. Our awareness that we are not yet what we could be is rooted in ideas of resurrection and new creation. Jesus used parables of growth and fulfilment, and the elusiveness of the coming Kingdom of God. There is a huge number of theological themes to be explored here, but I believe their main point of impact on our topic is as I have described it – the open-endedness of human existence before the creative and redeeming love of God.

This consciousness of unfulfilled potential is not an exclusively theological one, however, though I believe theology enormously illuminates it. All human beings, whether religiously aware or not, try to reach beyond themselves. All of us are shaped by our histories, and live, whether we believe it intellectually or not, as if we were free to create our own futures. All of us live in a variety of relationships with other people and have to acknowledge that what they are makes us in part what we are. A theological perspective enables this openness and these influences to be recognized in their ultimate form as receptiveness to the incessant creative activity of God, the God who holds us and all things in existence. If we want to know where to find the essence of our humanity, this surely is the right place to look. All the different dimensions of what it is to know a human being, from knowing their DNA sequence to knowing their personality, meet in this all-encompassing relationship with God. To see them this way sets them in perspective. The peril in not seeing them this way lies in imagining that we know more than we do.

I may seem to have spent too much time in stating the obvious. It is not news to anyone working in the field that our knowledge of these matters is limited. I have been concerned, though, to make the further point that it is inherently limited, in part because of the narrow focus of scientific enquiry, in part because of the nature of the processes which genetic structures initiate and in various degrees control, and in part because of the character of human life itself. This inherent limitation of our knowledge forms the background to what I now want to say on some of the practical issues which arise out of this work, and particularly on the dissemination of the information gained from it.

A scientific correspondent in an English newspaper recently wrote about people living with 'inherited genetic time bombs'. Time bombs are set irrevocably to explode. A sense of genetic inevitability hung heavily over his supposedly informed account of where this science is leading us. It seems to me essential, therefore, that at this most basic level of popular communication, the limitations of our knowledge should be emphasized again and again.

This is all the more urgent because of the widespread ignorance of science, which can make isolated statements about doom-laden scenarios seem all the more alarming. It is hard for many scientists to realize just how deep this ignorance is. Perhaps it is worse in my country than in the USA. Think, for example, of the implications of this piece of so-called 'general knowledge' in a commercially produced card game:

Question: 'What determines day and night?'
Answer: 'The rotation of the earth round the sun.'

Given that degree of popular scientific enlightenment, how many people are going to understand what geneticists can or cannot do, unless geneticists themselves, and those who write about them, avoid the kind of language which feeds misconceptions? Here are two more examples, both from scientific correspondents: the genome project is 'the key to understanding disease'. All disease? Again, the genetic code is 'the very stuff that determines human individuality' – which, to say the least, is bad luck on twins. Scientists themselves – apart from a handful of publicity seekers – are, for the most part, fairly humble about the extent of their knowledge, and that humility needs to be the starting-point in decisions about its use.

A sense of the inherent limitations of knowledge in this field should make us cautious about how such knowledge as we have is put to practical use. It is in this spirit that I now turn briefly to some of the practical questions, under three headings:

1. The effects of knowledge on those to whom it applies.
2. The possible misuse of that knowledge by others.
3. The therapeutic use of genetic knowledge.

1. The effects of knowledge on those to whom it applies

Most doctors have constantly to face the question whether to tell patients that they are likely to die. Up till a few decades ago the received wisdom in UK medicine was that on the whole patients should not be told. It may be that in the US with its much greater emphasis on knowing and publicizing all one's medical details, the received wisdom has been different, but I suspect not. The reasons usually given by those who believe in not telling were (a) the uncertainty of diagnosis (b) the danger that the patient might lose heart and give up the struggle and (c) the sheer difficulty of facing the truth, both for patient and doctor. Those who argued the opposite did so on the grounds that it is much better to face the truth than to hide from it, that those who are dying have a right to be allowed to prepare for death, especially if they have a religious faith, and that doctors have no right to hide knowledge from a patient unless it is obvious that disclosure would be cruel or harmful.

The fact that these latter arguments have on the whole prevailed suggests to me that it is probably wisest also to know the best or worst about one's genes, provided the information can be properly interpreted, and provided there is a proper recognition of the inherent limitations of this knowledge. Those who are told that they carry genetic risks are being given a chance to live in ways which will minimize such risks, both for themselves and for their families. But they need to be informed and open-eyed about the uncertainties. And they need to be aware of the danger of spreading an unnecessary blight over their lives, making them more anxious and less productive than they need be. There is also the danger of being seized by a belief in genetic determination which then becomes self-fulfilling. One of the trickiest aspects of genetic counselling must be in knowing how to balance an awareness of statistical probabilities against what I have described as the open-endedness of human nature, the personal resources for coping with an unlucky inheritance, when those resources cannot be measured in advance.

It is these unknown possibilities in human nature which persuade me that on the whole it is better to know the physical truth about oneself. But I believe that such knowledge should not be forced on people except in those cases where there is a high risk of passing on almost inevitable hereditary disease. There is an instructive parallel with AIDS. Blanket screening for HIV would be intrusive and wasteful. The anonymous screening of select groups gives vital information about the prevalence of HIV without intruding upon anybody's privacy. But it creates a huge ethical dilemma about whether positives so identified should be told, or whether they should be kept in ignorance with all the risks of infecting others. The voluntary testing of high risk groups, coupled with increasing hopes that something can actually be done for those identified, has proved in my country to be the most ethically acceptable policy, and the one most likely to produce results.

I believe the same is true for genetic testing. The useful operative principle would seem to be that when there are significant external indicators of genetic abnormality, then there should be a strong obligation to confirm this with actual genetic tests. But in the absence of such external indicators, there should be no such obligation. This way of approaching the matter has the merit of beginning with the whole person, with their family and medical history, membership of high risk groups, visible symptoms, rather than with their genes, with all the attendant uncertainties of projecting into the future what those genes might or might not do. To begin with genetics would surely be to practise medicine back to front. It would be to exacerbate the tendency to turn diagnostic tools into means of categorizing people, so progressively losing sight of the people themselves. There is a whole new range of ethical problems opening up at this point, the balance between concern for individuals and concern for populations. But I believe that to require involuntary testing in the absence of external indicators would be to subordinate the interests of individuals too much to those of the public at large.

2. The possible misuse of genetic knowledge

This is a much discussed topic, which goes far beyond the threats to privacy and the potential skewing of medicine to which I have already referred. When the WCC reported on biotechnology in 1989, stories of discrimination against individuals who had been genetically screened were a main focus of our concern. We heard horrifying stories from India and South Korea of the effects of pre-natal screening for sex selection. There were accounts of employees in large companies being compulsorily screened to provide information about their health prospects and about their ability to work in hostile environments. There is the ever-present problem when abortion is the only treatment on offer after pre-natal screening. There are fears that, given the increasing ability to diagnose major abnormalities at a very early stage, the minority who continue to be born with severe genetically based disablements will find themselves even more disadvantaged by the unspoken assumption that they ought not to have slipped through the net.

But perhaps the topic which illustrates most tellingly the dilemma caused by too much knowledge, is insurance. Successful insurance schemes depend on accurate statistical information about groups and relative ignorance about individuals. The relative ignorance about individuals is qualified by asking for certain information of a public and statistically assessable kind, age, occupation, health record, etc., but generally not by information about private habits and lifestyle. The question is, Where is it reasonable in insurance terms to draw the line? Too little information could expose insurance companies to exploitation by those who know that they carry high and undisclosed health risks. Too much information could increase discrimination against those who, through no fault of their own, are already disadvantaged. Since one of the purposes of insurance is to provide some counterbalance to 'the changes and chances of this mortal life', it could be argued on the basis of simple social justice that those with a fortunate genetic inheritance ought to bear some of the burdens of the less fortunate. This might mean drawing the line for insurance purposes between what I have already called the external indicators of health and circumstances, and the privileged and private knowledge of genetic make-up.

There is an obvious difficulty, however, in that some people's genetic abnormalities may already be known to insurers. There is also the principle of maximum honesty on which the integrity of insurance systems depends. Therefore, if some genetic information *can* be relevant for insurance purposes, and if all genetic information *might* be relevant, there will be strong pressure to insist on full genetic disclosure from everybody. But this would violate the principle I have expressed earlier, namely that in the absence of clear external indicators nobody should be forced to undergo genetic screening, or to know the results of it, should it be done involuntarily.

I suspect that this is a dilemma that can only be resolved by legislation. I am attracted by the idea of making genetic evidence inadmissible for insurance purposes, as has already been done, I believe, in California. And I would justify this on the three grounds, that external indicators of health are sufficient for insurance purposes, that the genetic information could add to the possibilities of unfair discrimination, and that such information should belong to the private and personal, such information should belong to the private and personal, not to the public realm. I shall return to this latter point in a moment.

3. The therapeutic use of genetic knowledge

Under this heading I need do no more than refer to the excellent Report of the Committee on the Ethics of Gene Therapy (the so-called 'Clothier Report') presented to Parliament in January 1992. The principles underlying it are set out as 'reverence for life and respect for the dignity and integrity of the person; the right to freedom and, especially in our context, a freedom of choice based on the right to knowledge; respect for privacy and the preservation of confidence; the importance in society of fairness and equity; and, casting its light over all, the quest for truth'.

Out of these convictions emerged three main recommendations:

(a) that although somatic cell gene therapy does not represent a major departure from established medical practice, it does pose new ethical challenges, and should therefore for the time being fall under the controls governing therapeutic research. In practice this means supervision of the procedures by local and national ethical committees;

(b) until the clinical procedures are better established, treatment by somatic cell gene therapy should be limited to those with life-threatening or otherwise very serious conditions for which no other treatment is available;

(c) no attempt should be made to modify human traits not associated with disease, nor should there be any attempts at germ line therapy.

At present these are only recommendations. I hope they will become regulations because, as I have already suggested in the case of insurance, we are moving into uncharted waters where ethical principles need to be given the backing of law if the flood of new knowledge and techniques is not to overwhelm our basic human values.

I return finally to those basic values, and in particular to the notion of privacy which underlies much of what I have been saying about the perils of trying to know too much. It is not a value which has had much prominence in Christian thinking. In fact there are those who dismiss it as a nineteenth-century cuckoo in the ethical nest, tainted by overtones of privilege, withdrawal from public accountability, secretiveness and unhealthy individualism. Politically-minded critics have described a concern for privacy as the essence of the bourgeois way of life. Religious critics have frequently been suspicious of an idea which seems to deny community values and smacks of indifference to others.

I grant that privacy is not unambiguously good. Yet the belief that there are things about a person which properly remain private seems to me a necessary part of the further belief that there is a core of human personality which should be inviolable. I have suggested earlier that ultimately that core is to be understood in terms of our individual relationship with God. It is a relationship which is never entirely separate from our relationship with others, but whether with God or with our fellow human beings, the essence of it is intimacy. Intimacy is the necessary setting within which we develop the confidence to be ourselves and to know ourselves at a deep level. And one of the major safeguards of such confidence, and protectors of intimate openness, is privacy. Privacy thus forms part of that cluster of values which surround the notion of respect for persons, and which locate the centre of ethics in claims about human transcendence of the merely physical.

Should we then seek to protect personal genetic information by assigning it to the realm of the private? Surely, it may be objected, among all possible pieces of information about a human life, personal genetic information is the most obviously and basically physico-chemical. Yet, and here lies the paradox in all this discussion, it also represents a foundational element in personal uniqueness; and it contains to an unknown degree some of the factors which will contribute to that person's destiny. While so much remains unknown it seems wisest not to separate our transcendent uniqueness too far from the physico-chemical uniqueness which in part undergirds it. Perhaps, as we learn more, and discern more clearly the boundaries of our inevitable ignorance in these matters, privacy about what we do know may seem less important. And so, paradoxically, by knowing more about our ignorance we may come to worry less about our genes.

Interlude

Cruelty to Animals

Sermon preached on the 150th Anniversary of the Society for the Prevention of Cruelty to Animals being granted the title of 'Royal SPCA' by Queen Victoria, Westminster Abbey, 4 October 1990

If the cat in the old nursery rhyme can go to London to look at a queen, it is also appropriate, surely, that a queen should look at a cat. Out of such mutual looking can develop a kind of mutual respect.

I hope this is not too frivolous a way to acknowledge the benefits of 150 years of royal patronage. The point is that the RSPCA has helped to change the way we look at things. And the fact that it has had an acknowledged and respected role in the life of the nation has been an important element in this process of change.

So today we give thanks for what has been achieved; for the steady growth of the Society; for the huge weight of suffering prevented and relieved; for the new sensitivities now enshrined in the law; for the tireless and courageous work of the inspectors; for the enthusiasm and dedication of the many local branches; for the spread of the work in many other parts of the world.

We give thanks, too, on this the feast of St Francis, for the Christian inspiration which led to the formation of the Society, and has helped to maintain it; and our worship reminds us of the long history of Christian concern for animals, not alas a universally acknowledged concern and not expressed even in our day as strongly as it might be. But it is there. And where better than in Westminster Abbey can we affirm that God loves all his creatures, and bids us to respect them and to care about the quality of their lives.

As members of the Society will know only too well, it is easy to say these things and hard to work them out in practice. You will know too that even while we give thanks for what has been achieved, revolting forms of cruelty are still horrifyingly widespread, and new forms of dominating animal life and bending it to human purposes are still being devised. The Society is needed as much as it ever was. But throughout its long history it has been wise, I believe, to steer a middle course between various extremes, recognizing that the whole question of our relationship with the animal world is still full of unresolved tensions.

This does not make for ready agreement on charting the way ahead. There will be those who want to push further and further in the direction of acknowledging animal rights as in some sense virtually on a par with human rights. There will be others for whom that kind of language seems extravagant or even absurd, and who are mostly concerned with the elimination of obvious abuses. Arguments and even conflicts between those involved in animal welfare are not surprising, nor do they invalidate the cause. They spring directly out of the ambiguities which are part of our history.

On the one hand we depend on animals; sometimes directly as for food or as pets; sometimes indirectly as for medicine or for the maintenance of the environment. The uncomfortable truth is that as a human race we have got where we are by exploiting the rest of creation, and particularly our brothers and sisters the animals.

On the other hand, we cannot be happy with this history. Many people feel increasingly guilty about it. We are aware of how disastrously we have undervalued the quality of much animal life, and underestimated the capacity of animals to feel suffering. Our looking at animals has taught us to see ourselves differently, no longer as lords and masters but as in some sense members of the same family.

There are deep theological issues underlying these changing perceptions. How are we to understand ourselves as creatures made in the image of God? What kind of responsibility does this give us in sharing God's concern for the rest of creation?

> Lord, help me try
> To love the fly

is a prayer which is not yet on everybody's lips. But it is encouraging that our human role within the created order is now an active area of theological study. And I hope the Christian Churches, and other religions too, will increasingly be seen as a resource for those who are dealing with the sharp end of the problems in the face of actual abuse. I hope, too, that inevitable disagreements will be seen as a necessary part of the process of learning who we are and what we must do in this world whose ecological horizons have been expanding so rapidly.

Meanwhile, the Society has probably been wise to concentrate on the prevention of cruelty. Cruelty is directly observable. We know deep inside ourselves that it is wrong. We can appeal to a single moral principle that preventable suffering ought to be prevented. And we can avoid, I hope, the sophisticated twist in the argument which says that cruelty is wrong because it brutalizes the perpetrator. No doubt it does. But it is wrong fundamentally because it causes suffering.

But even this simple moral basis for your work has its complications. We tend to be more moved by the suffering of animals which make sounds resembling the human voice. Crying, screaming, whining tear at our heart strings, as do large soulful eyes. Fewer people are moved by the suffering of rats. And do fish suffer? There's an explosive question. And how should we rate the suffering of animals denied their proper habitat or means of expression when it is claimed that they must be happy because they are eating?

Bit by bit we are being led to see that though cruelty is the necessary starting-point, there is a deeper shift of perspective required. We have to accept that animal life, all animal life, is to be valued and respected, not just for our sake, but for its own sake, and ultimately for God's sake. We have to dispel the idea that the creation exists exclusively for us. This doesn't mean we can't use it, and can't use animals within proper limits, for our own purposes. We have to as the condition of our survival. But we do so as partners in the business of being alive, aiming to enhance rather than to exploit, conscious of our dependence on one another in a world loved and valued by God.

When the cat looked at the queen it saw in its cattishness what it was best fitted to see – the mouse under the chair. We, conscious of a royal perspective, must see further than that. The animal kingdom has its own dignity and integrity, and its own special place in the Kingdom of God.

Do pigs have wings?

Diocesan Newspaper, July 1992

There is a well-known story about Father Kelly, Founder of the Society of the Sacred Mission, who said to a friend visiting Kelham: 'Come and I will show you my proofs of the existence of God.' His story goes on: 'Then I showed him our pigs. I love pigs. They are so delightfully ugly, and so blissfully self-satisfied over it. A fat old sow came slowly waddling towards us, with its two huge ears – like Macbeth's dagger – pointing the way that she should go. And my friend looked puzzled. "Oh, yes," I replied, "if I had shown you stars, flowers, a sunset, you would have said, 'Ah! how true!' but I do not greatly need God in order to see that beautiful things are beautiful and – well, elevating. I do want to hear of a God who can find a beauty and a joy and an eternal value in my poor pigs. If God also laughs softly over their funniness, I do not mind that. I do it too!"'

I was reminded of the story after reading a spate of newspaper articles about God, his nature, his existence or non-existence, and the general mess religious people have made of trying to explain what he is like. The articles were full of elevated comments on big bangs, and knowing the mind of God through physics, and whether black holes and evolutionary computer games have made him unnecessary.

But that is not where most people start in thinking about God. They are much more likely to start, if not with pigs, with some other familiar but puzzling aspect of ordinary life in which they look for meaning. Religion in its simplest terms is about making sense of life, this life first of all, and particularly those aspects of it which challenge and disturb us. This is why suffering and ways of responding to it have always been such central religious themes. Undeserved happiness bubbling to the surface in thanksgiving is another familiar religious experience. There is also the pervading sense of depth and mysteriousness in some of our encounters with other human beings, a depth which gives substance to the idea that personality itself has roots in some transcendent reality.

I cite these examples, not as arguments for God, but as pointers to the way in which a sense of the presence of God communicates itself. Insights of this kind can be used to give clues to a framework of meaning, which in turn enlarges our ability to cope in a meaningful way with other ranges of experience, and with the kind of choices life throws at us.

What I have described in terms of personal experience can be seen writ large in the Bible story. Much of it can be read as a struggle to make sense of a tumultuous history in the belief that the hand of God can be discerned in it. The fact that this belief survived numerous disasters, disappointments and criticisms is evidence of how strongly based it was in the lives of those who went through these experiences. Appeal, as in many of the Psalms, to the miracle of the exodus some five hundred years after it had happened, would not have cut much ice unless those who made it were themselves experiencing their God as the God who could and would rescue them too. Nor nowadays can appeal to the resurrection, simply as a historical fact some two thousand years ago, carry full conviction unless there are those whose own lives witness to Christ's risen power today. Great biblical events may shape and inspire ordinary daily life. But it is within ordinary life, puzzling over pigs, bringing up children, wondering where the money goes, that the daily walk with God takes place.

This is not to say that black holes and all that are irrelevant; but they are not a point at which religion really touches most of us. If we have given up trying to understand what on earth – or in heaven – a black hole is, the quality of our life will not greatly suffer.

But who is this God who walks beside us through the ordinary things of life? Here I want to say a word to those for whom the conventional Christian answer seems inaccessible, often for a whole variety of reasons. Our language about God has become devalued. Too many terrible atrocities have been committed in the name of the Churches. Christians speak with different voices. Our lives throw doubt on our words. The modern world has no room for this God who no longer seems to be needed by science as an explanation. The objections could go on and on.

And yet . . . why is our world so obsessed with God? Why does faith persist, even in the face of such an unsavoury history? Why have generations of people struggled, suffered, died and laid the whole burden of their hopes on this word 'God'? Why is God still headline news even in our secularized press? Because despite the abuses, misuses, misunderstandings, and even murders committed in the name of God, the vast majority of human beings are unwilling, I believe properly unwilling, to conclude that life has no meaning outside itself.

Ivan in Dostoevsky's *The Brothers Karamazov* says: 'What's strange is not that God should really exist; the marvel is that such an idea, the idea of the necessity of God, could enter the head of such a savage, vicious beast as man. So holy it is, so touching, so wise.' To put the same point in abstract terms, belief in God has lain at the centre of human consciousness because it is the focus of meaning around which morality, emotion and understanding have been held together. Remove it, and the world begins to fragment.

Christians would want to say much more than this. But it is only possible to hear and respond to the gospel when we know our need of it, and when we are no longer blinded by the dust which history has thrown up. When that moment comes, the heart of the gospel proves to be surprisingly simple. John 3.16 is one favourite way of putting it. Here is another, by R.E.C. Browne, a wonderful preacher it was once my privilege to know: 'At a fixed point in time God became Man without ceasing to be God, that men might become Godly without ceasing to be men.'

Pigs remain obstinately wingless. They fulfil God's purpose by being what they are. But the human spirit was born to fly.

PART

3

Rights and Responsibilities

9

Human Nature and Human Rights

The Gore Lecture, delivered in Westminster Abbey, 9 November 1988

I have a nasty feeling that Charles Gore might not have approved the title of this lecture. It is true that he was concerned about human nature; indeed that is the title of one of his Gifford Lectures in *The Philosophy of the Good Life*. But the lecture is mostly taken up with a defence of human freedom against determinism. It is true also that he was deeply concerned about those moral standards which he saw as lying at the basis of any and every good life and good society. But he only incidentally referred to human rights in extensive writing on social and ethical questions, and it may be instructive to ask why this is so.

I want to suggest, and this is a large part of the thesis of this lecture, that the language of human rights emerged and belongs within the context of political struggle. It belongs, at least in the form in which it originated in the West, to situations where individuals are attempting to assert some autonomy, some breathing space for themselves, over against political or religious powers or social forces which are experienced as oppressive, suffocating, or stagnant. Rights are asserted where people's developing self-image clashes with the image imposed on them by circumstances. What this dependence on context says about their validity we shall have to see as we go on.

Meanwhile let me illustrate. Societies rooted in traditionalism, no matter what part of the world we study, seem to have had no place for the concept of rights. Where inherited thought forms and patterns of behaviour have been strong, dissent may have been expressed, but usually not in terms of rights. The Bible, for instance, despite its revolutionary potential, says virtually nothing about them. True, there are many ingenious theological arguments which try to repair the deficiency. I have heard it argued that since the Bible says a great deal about obligations it must also be saying a great deal about rights, rights and obligations being two sides of the same coin. I wonder what Isaiah and Jeremiah, not to mention St Paul, would have made of that. Moltmann in a much-quoted essay draws on the whole biblical tradition as grounding fundamental human rights in what he calls rather obscurely 'God's right to man'. But this is not the point. It may be possible to *deduce* some rights from biblical teaching; but it is a mistake to say that the Bible is *about* human rights, because that implies commitment to a concept and a way of thinking which did not then exist.

Nor did it exist in medieval times, though once again there was a strong theological background, the idea of universal moral law, which could have been, but was not, expressed in 'rights' language. The fact is that the fundamental concept of rights is humanistic in origin. It made its first appearance during the Renaissance, and achieved classic form during the Enlightenment. It inspired the revolutionary struggles in the latter part of the eighteenth century, legitimized them, and gained fresh impetus from them. It came back into prominence in the aftermath of the Second World War when the full horrors of totalitarianism had become apparent – a vivid reality for us on this fiftieth anniversary of *Kristalnacht*. And since the UN Declaration of Human Rights, forty years ago this year, the concept of rights has provided the vocabulary and much of the motivation for liberation movements, reform movements, and humanitarian efforts in every part of the world.

The language belongs within a context, characteristically the context of emancipation. Gore did not use it, because his world, even as late as 1929, was different. He lived in a society which in many ways had still not felt the full force of modern turbulence.

He must also have been conscious of the strong sense of unease among Christians about the concept of rights, even when its origins in a self-confident and sometimes arrogant humanism have been discounted. Belief in providence, like belief in fate, militates against the assertion of rights. There is a perpetual conflict in the Christian soul between the acceptance of suffering and the struggle against it. There is a reluctance to give rein to the self-assertiveness and personal acquisitiveness which seem inseparable from some claims to human rights. And, most tellingly of all, there is a sense of the primacy of duty, a sense which was particularly strong in Gore himself.

In fact there need be no conflict between rights and duties. Tom Paine in *The Rights of Man* refers to a member of the French National Assembly who made precisely this point in 1789. And having quoted the Declaration of Human Rights, Paine himself added: 'A declaration of rights is, by reciprocity, a declaration of duties also. Whatever is my right as a man is also the right of another; and it becomes my duty to guarantee as well as to possess.' The point was put succinctly in the chapter heading of a recent book, 'Your Rights are my Responsibility'.[1]

But this reciprocity can easily be lost, especially when rights are seen as individual, and responsibilities are diffused through an amorphous entity called society, or directed unerringly towards the government. If the proper balance between rights and responsibilities becomes skewed, then indeed Christians have reason to fear that too much talk of rights dangerously inverts the gospel priorities.

There is a further problem, and not only for Christians, in the tendency of rights to proliferate. The list of purported rights grows longer and longer. What begin as wants and interests quickly become elevated into needs and claims, and ultimately into full-blown rights. The so-called right to have children is a case in point. There is no doubt that the majority of people want to have children. There is also no doubt that, for a variety of reasons including strong social pressures, this want can become a pressing need, so pressing that it can be destructive if it is not satisfied. But when do strong needs become the basis of rights? It would be reasonable to argue that if a state set impediments against having children, as happened in both India and China, then a right to procreate could be claimed against an abuse of government authority. But is this an unrestricted right, no matter what the population problems? Or consider the case when the impediment is not external but internal or personal. Is there a right to medical treatment to alleviate childlessness, and if so how far does it extend? Do single women have a right to bear children whether or not they intend to provide a normal home background?

I simply list these questions as a reminder of how far the language of rights has moved into fields where the ethical issues are complex, and where it is not at all clear that claims to have rights are of much help in resolving them. In the classic confrontation between Tom Paine and Edmund Burke, Burke summed up the difficulty very sharply. Too much talk of rights, he said, arouses desires which cannot be satisfied. In our own day, a proliferation of claimed rights can be accused of adding to the general discontent.

So far I have skated over the familiar distinction between individual and social rights. I have assumed the Western tradition in which rights are essentially about individual freedom, and that this sets their context in terms of individual assertion over against a society seen as oppressive or in other ways limiting. The classic declarations of human rights are mostly in this form, and stem from such thinkers as Locke and Paine whose philosophical starting-point is the individual. In statements concerning these fundamental human rights, the individual is stripped of all that locates him or her in society. Everyone is entitled to them, we are told in the UN Declaration, 'without distinction of any kind, such as race, colour, sex, language, religion, political or other opinion, national or social origin, property, birth or other status'. Who would want to quarrel with that? The point about rights is that they are universal. But this stripping away of all distinctions has a curious side-effect. It can encourage a view of human beings as bare autonomous selves abstracted from all those differentiations and relationships which actually make human beings interesting, significant and individual.

The social interpretation of rights corrects this. Eastern bloc advocates give primacy to the conditions of life which make human flourishing possible, the right to work, the right to education, the right to an equitable standard of living. Such rights are more overtly political than individual rights, but it is claimed that without them individual freedom has no real substance. I may in theory be free to take any job I like, but the freedom is meaningless if there are no jobs available.

This tradition of social rights is one of the many legacies from Rousseau, who saw the fundamental problem of politics as finding 'a form of association in which each while uniting himself with all, may still obey himself alone, and remain as free as before'. It avoids, even if Rousseau himself does not, the egotism and the ultimate emptiness of the 'free autonomous self' tradition: but it carries its own dangers. Consider this quotation: 'The rights of the individual are today not worth serious criticism . . . The welfare of the community is the end and is the ultimate standard. And over its members the right of its moral organism is absolute. Its duty and its right is to dispose of those members as it seems best.'

Who said that? Stalin? Hitler? Marx? It was an English Idealist philosopher, one of the mentors of William Temple, F. H. Bradley, who took up Rousseau's concept of 'the general will' of society, gave it a Hegelian twist, and then pursued it to its logical conclusion. Social rights can swallow up individual rights as recent history only too painfully teaches us.

Gore, I am glad to say, would have none of this. On the whole it has been in the best Christian tradition to refuse this opposition between individual and social rights, but rather to see them as necessary complements to one another. A Christian understanding of human life is necessarily both personal and social. The Eastern Orthodox tradition has always known this and has expressed it most characteristically by seeing the image of God in man as somehow reflecting the complex inner life of the Trinity. Our Western theological tradition has gone through greater fluctuations and it is not hard to see how Protestant ideas about individual salvation find their secular counterpart in ideas about the isolated autonomous self. But in recent years traditions in these matters have been converging, and I doubt whether many Christians now would dissent from the classic Roman Catholic statement on human rights in Pope John XXIII's encyclical *Pacem in Terris*. It roots the idea of human rights in the fundamental dignity given to each individual by God, but then goes on:

Since men are social by nature they are meant to live with others and work for another's welfare. A well-ordered society requires that men recognize and observe their mutual rights and duties. It also demands that each contribute generously to the establishment of a civic order in which rights and duties are more sincerely and effectively acknowledged and secured.

Thus far I have spoken rather critically about human rights. I have described the uncongenial origins of rights language; its dependence on particular political and social contexts; its excesses and distortions. I have dwelt on the difficulty Christians have often found in reconciling advocacy of human rights with more traditional attitudes and modes of expression. And I have referred to the different traditions concerning rights which have played a significant part in the mutual incomprehension between East and West. It is important to come to terms with these difficulties if we are to go on to say, as I believe we must, that the advocacy of human rights is indispensable in our modern world, and is a duty laid upon us as Christians. But if we are to do this we need much greater clarity than exists at present about what human rights are and on what they are based.

First, though, why are they so necessary? There are the obvious political reasons in a world where so many abuses cry out for remedy. It is a world where increasing numbers of people are conscious of how lives are lived elsewhere and of the possibilities of change; easy communications have seen to that. But it is also a world which through its sheer complexity, its interrelatedness and its concentrations of power can be extraordinarily resistant to change. Everybody knows about massive worldwide poverty. Nobody knows how to eradicate it without creating another range of equivalent problems. So there has to be a language, a language to express the hopes and the frustrations, a language to ensure that the problems do not drop out of sight, a language which can exert both moral and political pressure. This is what human rights language does. And it gains immeasurable force by its claim to be universal. Rights which belong to human beings as such, whether conceived individually or socially or both together, can be pressed as overriding all other considerations, all excuses, all displays of power, and can do so in theory with the support of the whole international community. Hobbes put the opposite point of view when, in describing government by analogy with a game he wrote: 'When nothing else is turned up, clubs are trumps.' The claim made by advocates of human rights is that in advance of every other principle, moral or political, rights are trumps.

Let me dwell for a moment on their universality. It not only gives them power; it makes them accessible and brings them within everybody's grasp. It is a point Christians need to take seriously. We are always in danger of saying our own Christian thing in our own language and on the basis of our own particular theological justifications, with the result that we are heard only within our own inner circle. On some occasions this may be right. I am not denying the value of Christian distinctiveness. But there are times when we are too easily content to be ineffective. If there is a language to hand that, without undermining the gospel, can be used in the service of justice, and that can unite us across the barriers of religion, culture and nationality, then it is faithless to turn our backs on it.

This is one reason why I was concerned that the bishops at the Lambeth Conference should do a little thinking about rights; and they did indeed reaffirm the UN Declaration, though without, alas, carrying the thinking any further. This awareness of the necessity for Christians to learn to use the concept of rights also underlay a project in which I have been marginally involved for the past few years, and which has now come to birth in a book entitled *Human Rights and Responsibilities in Britain and Ireland*.[2] Central to the project was the attempt to find some common ground, particularly in relation to Northern Ireland, on which people of different religious convictions might agree, and by this means to make small advances in removing feelings of injustice and building up trust. By concentrating on rights and responsibilities we were able to overcome many of the usual theological and cultural divisions. We were able to produce a book which was at least not rejected by the contending interested parties in Britain and Ireland. And some of its recommendations have already been put into effect.

Human rights language can actually work; and part of its

effectiveness derives from its universality. But now it is time to draw another distinction before coming to the major questions, What *are* human rights? and, On what are they based? The distinction is between rights as enshrined in law, and rights seen as prior to law, indeed as the foundation of law.

The book to which I have just been referring took a rather narrow view of human rights. It defined them as those rights which have been declared and ratified in international law and to which appeal can therefore be made, not simply on the basis of their inherent justice, but on the basis of obligations which nations have actually undertaken. In practical terms such a legally based view of rights has obvious advantages. It cuts out some of the argument; it provides a degree of clarity and definiteness which is often lacking in moral claims; and in some circumstances there is even a rudimentary legal apparatus whereby claims can be settled. Nothing I say hereafter should be construed as in any way devaluing this highly significant post-war development in international law.

Nevertheless it is essential not to confine our concern for human rights to these legally based and internationally recognized rights, for two main reasons. First, because the most difficult issues concerning human rights lie at the frontiers of law where the law is either not observed, or not developed enough to be helpful. Secondly, and this is the really fundamental point, because concentrating on legally based rights alone confuses the distinction between possessing rights and having those rights recognized and implemented. Black South Africans possess rights as human beings whatever the South African government may say or do. In a different, legal, sense they do not possess some of the rights which ordinary citizens might expect to enjoy. Their appeal against oppressive laws which deprive them of legal rights is in the name of inherent rights which they possess regardless of those laws. They would also want to argue, surely, that these inherent rights do not just depend on international law seen as somehow transcending South African law, but on some basic truth about themselves as human beings. Indeed it is precisely when human rights are *not* legally recognized or enforced that the language of rights is at its most urgent, and needs to be at its most universal.

In a country where rights are enjoyed as a normal part of

life, not much is said about them, and it is possible for such well-placed politicians to look askance at some of the more extravagant claims made by international bodies, and not least by the WCC. In such a country, rights are generally enshrined in a mass of legislation covering everything from police procedures to data protection. The specificity of law adds to its effectiveness, whereas by contrast appeals from it to some more general principle, as set out, say, in the UN Declaration, are likely to be messy and inconclusive. Such appeals function as the last resort, or bottom line, when things are going seriously wrong. What are likely to be even more messy and inconclusive are appeals beyond codified rights to general moral rights, and there are therefore great pressures to reduce the areas in which such appeals might be effective. As one who from time to time has to administer discipline I am always very reluctant to go above and beyond the law in the name of some claimed right; too many such appeals make the administration of law unworkable.

But this understandable reluctance must not be allowed to mask the truth that law depends on morality, and not vice versa: and nationally or internationally acknowledged human rights depend on something which belongs to human beings as such, and not vice versa; and furthermore concern for human rights is more usually a sign of their non-implementation than of their embodiment in the assumptions and institutions of a particular nation or culture. As I said at the beginning of this lecture, human rights language belongs most character- istically within the context of political struggle.

But what *are* rights? and on what are they based? They purport to be more than strong moral claims. It would be true rather to say that they *exert* strong moral claims. They are an attempt to pinpoint some basic feature of being human which has profound consequences for the way human beings ought to treat one another. The question is, Does any such feature exist, and if so, what is it?

There have been many attempts to identify it. 'Human dignity' is a phrase much used in this context. Unfortunately it does not advance the argument very far. To ascribe dignity to human beings, and to ascribe rights to them, are perilously close to two ways of saying the same thing. Neither makes clear the other's basis.

But surely, says the Christian, the human dignity which undergirds human rights is a reflection of the image of God. Our rights and our very being depend on the worth God places on us by having put his own image within us. This is a second, much-used argument, and in a Christian context it must carry great weight. It is certainly a reason for Christians to take the concept of rights very seriously, though I suspect it holds difficulties for those who want to underscore the reality of original sin. If God's image in us is marred, how can we deduce from it what properly belongs to our fundamental nature as human beings?

But, there is much broader difficulty than that. Universal rights have to be based on something which is not only universal, as we believe the image of God in all people to be, but which is perceived and accepted as universal – and that sadly, the image of God certainly is not. Thus a purely Christian defence of human rights fails at precisely the point where it is most needed.

An alternative approach might be through an analysis of human needs. This too has been much explored though without great success. At first sight it might seem relatively easy to draw up a list of the basic conditions and provisions which allow human beings to flourish. No doubt each of us could do it for ourselves. The difficulty is that after describing basic needs for the maintenance of life itself, our lists would begin to diverge. One characteristic of the 'good life', as Gore was well aware when he wrote his Gifford lectures, is its enormous diversity, and this begins to show itself even at the level of quite basic needs. Is the need for privacy, for example, basic to our humanity, or a modern fad? In theory, therefore, a needs-based approach to human rights might succeed in establishing them. In practice, it doesn't. And in any case I have already, in referring to the modern tendency for rights to proliferate, made the point that needs and rights are different.

What about natural law? This too seems at first sight quite promising. Indeed the title of this lecture might suggest that this is the point towards which my argument is leading. 'Human nature and human rights' has a satisfying roundness to it. Furthermore the great merit of a natural law approach is that it can be Christian while at the same time it applies to everybody. Natural law is in theory natural to human beings, whatever their beliefs; the exercise of reason, with perhaps a little help from the Church, ought to be sufficient to disclose it.

Once again, though, this is easier said than done, however desirable it might be. Christians have strong reasons for wanting to believe that there are truths about the order of nature, including human nature, which somehow reflect the mind and intention of God. But we have not succeeded in persuading the secular world that there are. Educated people are too conscious nowadays of how deeply our perceptions have been conditioned by history, by our social circumstances, by unacknowledged beliefs and prejudices, and of how hard it is to stand back from all this and say anything about human nature as such. We are also conscious of living in an evolving world where the idea of some fixed entity called 'human nature' fits oddly with the rest of what we know about human development.

The evidence is not all one-sided. There is evidence of convergence as well as divergence in the understanding of what it is to be human. There are some basic moral imperatives, like the need to love one another, which ring true across the ages and across the cultures. But the more these are spelt out in concrete terms the greater the scope for disagreement. The sad truth is that natural law has by and large failed as an instrument for securing universal moral agreement. It therefore fails to offer a secure basis for universal rights. Indeed the same could be said of every attempt to argue rationally and empirically for anything but the most bland and general statement about the value of persons.

Where does that then leave us? It begins to look as if the talk of rights has no firm rational foundation. Bentham called rights 'nonsense on stilts'. Alasdair MacIntyre sums up their history like this:

> The best reason for asserting so bluntly that there are no such rights is indeed of precisely the same type as the best reason which we possess for asserting that there are no witches and the best reason which we possess for asserting that there are no unicorns: every attempt to give good reasons for asserting that there *are* such rights has failed.[3]

Here is our dilemma. Our world needs, and needs desperately, to believe in human rights. It has enshrined many of them in law. It needs some basis for regarding them as universally valid. And it needs, too, some way of distinguishing supposed rights from those which can actually receive some kind of validation. Yet reason and argument cannot take us there.

Perhaps we need a different view of what people are; and a different view of what rights are. Let me take you back to Tom Paine, quoting La Fayette: 'Call to mind the sentiments . . . engraved in the heart of every citizen, and which take a new force when they are recognized by all. For a nation to love liberty, it is sufficient that she knows it; to be free, it is sufficient that she wills it.'

Note the emphasis on recognizing, and knowing, and willing. There is a dynamic in human rights language which goes beyond the assertion of some general principle, some rational conclusion, and actually grasps hold of new possibilities. Maybe we are not talking about something inherent in human nature at all, but about something human beings can aspire to, create, discover, will, work towards, precisely because human nature is not fixed, static, given once and for all, but open-ended, always capable of further growth, full of further potential.

Such a view would certainly make sense of much of the history of human rights in which new rights are constantly being discovered, or perhaps invented, as the frontiers of human awareness expand and the sense of our human interdependence increases.

There are also theological attractions in thinking of human rights mainly in terms of hopes and aspirations for the future. An Australian theologian, John Henley, has expressed it like this: 'There remains a further possibility of rights which are truly human, not so much because of what human beings already are and can be known to be, as because of who and what they may yet be, a possibility which is eschatological.'[4]

Rights grounded in a theology of hope might be more true to the gospel and less vulnerable to the usual theological objections than rights grounded in the notion of obligation. 'It does not yet appear what we shall be . . .' but we can make claims for the future, both for ourselves and for others, because we know that by God's grace 'what shall be' can transcend both the frustrations and the complacencies of the present.

Putting it another way, to claim a right, on this view, is to make a bid for a more fully human self and a more fully human world, with the implication that self and world are involved, under God, in the process of mutual creation. We shape our world and are shaped by it; but we can also dream dreams about what it might be. And when those dreams are enshrined in acknowledged rights humanity as a whole is strengthened. Of course, we may make mistakes. Eschatology lacks the certainty of history. But it is no less Christian for depending on faith.

The word 'faith', however, should set the alarm bells ringing. If an eschatological interpretation of rights has in the end to depend on discovery and adventurousness, hope backed by faith, what chance is there of winning acceptance for it beyond the community of faith? What happens to the quest for universality?

I believe there is a secular rational ground for holding to a forward-looking view of human rights, and hence that the quest for universality may not be as hopeless as it seems. We have already seen the problem in trying to identify particular aspects or qualities of human nature as a basis for rights. These are all mutable and disputable. People can argue for ever about what human nature is.

Nevertheless there is one quality of being human which is not to be discounted on these grounds, because it underlies them. This is precisely the quality of open-endedness. Human beings contain untapped possibilities. We are mysteries, even to ourselves.

Furthermore, there is one aspect of being human which has to underlie every statement made about human morality. This is the claim that human beings are moral agents. Each of us has a moral responsibility in his or her own way to become more fully human. And because there is a realm of possibility which is not prescribed in advance, there must be a bewildering variety of ways of doing this.

Put these two thoughts together – moral agency and open-endedness – and it becomes possible to say something about being human which has universal validity, yet leaves open the question of precisely what fulfilled humanity entails. The characteristics of human fulfilment have to be discovered rather than deduced. The sheer fact of being human invites us to just the kind of moral adventure which Christian faith presents to us in terms of the eschatology of hope.

Assertions of human rights are significant steps in this adventure. They are instructions on the road to developing a more human and humane world. They represent hard-won insights into what is humanly possible, and what can by experience be shown to enhance the responsible and open-ended quality of human life. Some rights safeguard the bottom line of what it is to be human.

The moral and legal establishment of actual rights no doubt has to entail moral argument and rational decision-making. I have already referred to the complexity of any supposed 'right to have children', and the need to draw careful distinctions. But the assertion of human rights is not identical with moral argument and rational decision-making. It may draw, and I suspect in the past has frequently drawn, on concealed religious assumptions. It may, and frequently does, include elements of moral intuition and prophecy. An American author, Jack Donnelly, has described rights as 'self fulfilling prophecies'. Believe in them, and they change you, and change the world. He goes on to spell out their mixture of utopianism and realism. I quote: 'Human rights doctrines say in effect, "Treat a person like a human being and you'll get one". But they also say "Here's *how* you treat someone as a human being" and proceed to enumerate a list of human rights which establish a framework within which a government must act.'[5]

This forward-looking interpretation of rights, whether expressed in secular or theological terms, may help us to understand two features of rights to which I have several times referred in this lecture: first their dependence on context, and secondly their tendency to proliferate.

If assertions of rights represent the leading edge of moral insight, then proliferation is inevitable. This is not to say that every such assertion is sustainable or that every supposed right should be regarded as such. The leading edge is where the moral battles have to be fought, and even if a moral battle is won it may not be appropriate to translate the fruits of it into the language of rights. I would like myself to impose a test on any claim to a new human right, namely the question, 'Who precisely has the responsibility for upholding and implementing it?' Nevertheless rights will proliferate, and properly so, as we learn from one another and advance in our understanding of what it is to be human.

But only what I have called 'the bottom line of human rights' will be truly universal. The remainder will depend on context, on what is perceived as possible within a given society, on the places where the shoe pinches and injustice is manifest. The rights which actually concern particular people will differ from society to society and from one time to another. By claiming universality, however, even for a limited range of rights, a basic sense of the possibilities of human flourishing can be fed into the bloodstream of a society, with who knows what results.

Let me end by returning to some words I have already quoted from Jack Donnelly: 'Treat a person like a human being and you'll get one.' It is not the whole of the gospel, nor is it the whole of politics and social wisdom. But it is a good start. Christians can surely hear the echoes in it of the graciousness of God who treats us beyond our deserving in order to lead us beyond our imagining. I think Gore would have approved of that.

Notes

1. Sydney D. Bailey (ed.), *Human Rights and Responsibilities in Britain and Ireland*. Macmillan 1988.
2. ibid.
3. A. MacIntyre, *After Virtue* (Duckworth 1981), p. 67.
4. J. Henley, 'Theology and the Basics of Human Rights' (*Scottish Journal of Theology*, vol. 39 [1986]), p. 375.
5. Jack Donnelly, *The Concept of Human Rights* (Croom Helm 1985), p. 33.

10

Finding a Moral Heart for Europe

Lecture delivered at St George's House, Windsor, 5 June 1992

The events of the past few days make me wonder whether my title ought to be 'creating a moral heart for Europe', or perhaps even 'hoping' for one. But I stick to 'finding' because, despite the many dissatisfactions with the European Community, there is and always has been a moral vision at its heart. It was present in 1943 when Jean Monnet wrote the prophetic note which was to set the essential terms of all that was to follow: 'The allies won the first world war and then lost the peace. They are going to win the second world war. The question is, can we win the peace? There is only one way: treat Germany on a basis of equality and begin to be responsible jointly for the production of coal and steel.'

The moral vision was peace and mutual responsibility. Economic interdependence was the means, not the end. Monnet himself was absolutely clear about this. He is recorded as saying:

The real change we are after is not the free flow of goods. It's the change in the relation between people, and this change comes about because these people are no longer simply thinking in terms of their national, limited responsibilities, my responsibilities over against those of someone else. They are now thinking about their common joint responsibilities. This is the revolutionary thing we are trying to do, the revolutionary character of the process of change that we are trying to set in motion. That process is a revolution, and should be never-ending.

It is not surprising that this moral vision came out of a country reflecting on the reasons for its defeat. One of the odder characters enlisted to start this process of reflection was Simone Weil who worked in London with Monnet's subsequent collaborator, Maurice Schumann: she had written a brilliant analysis of what was wrong with Europe, and especially with France, in the years between the wars. Her later wartime book, *The Need for Roots*, was described by T. S. Eliot as the sort of book the young ought to read before they lose their capacity for thought by becoming involved in politics. What is interesting about it, for our purposes, is her emphasis on human obligations and needs, and her criticism of human rights as encouraging an unhealthy self-concern. It was not a fashionable thing to say, and nobody took much notice. But I like to think that the vision of Europe as a sharing of obligations and a concern for each other's needs owes something to this strange twentieth-century saint.

The difficulties arise when the obligations are spelt out in detail. I suspect that one reason for popular disillusionment with the European vision is that up till now the main impact of the Community has been through the attempt to create an absurdly level playing-field for the Market. The character of the whole thing has been that of nit-picking bureaucracy, whereas the few opportunities to inspire a wider vision in response to real needs have been muffed. I think here of the muted European response to the Gulf War, and to the current environmental concerns. There is a wariness about co-operation, in part the product of a growing sense of the enormous complexity of the concept of Europe; and this includes fundamental disagreements about where the borders of Europe should be drawn. If the acceptance of mutual obligations is to help us find what Jacques Delors has called 'a spiritual foundation for Europe' we need to ask deeper questions about what Europe is.

It has never had fixed borders. In fact Europe has usually

defined itself in cultural rather than in geographical terms – Christendom over against Islam and barbarianism; Western over against Eastern civilization. And now in the post-colonial era it is the cultural aspects of European civilization that create for us such a complex relationship with other continents.

J. M. Roberts in an introductory essay for the 1991 Malvern Conference has described four features of European civilization which, for good or ill, have shaped the modern world: 'its sheer power; its focus in the idea of the individual; its unique relationship with science and technology; its self-critical character'.

1. The sheer power has been obvious, militarily in wars of conquest and wars of self-destruction; but also culturally and economically, and through such effective signs of cultural power as covering the world with railways and transistor radios. The fact that most of the latter are now manufactured in Japan makes them no less 'Western'; it simply makes Japan more Western.

2. Europe's focus on the idea of the individual is a legacy, partly of the Reformation and partly of the Enlightenment. It has been liberating, at times revolutionary, but also destructive of forms of community life which has given other civilizations their stability. The present concern of the Churches with *koinonia* – communion – as a key theological concept has been an attempt to redress the balance. This strand of Christian thinking, predominantly but not exclusively Catholic, is constantly making the point that though we are persons with individual dignity and human rights, we also belong together and only find our true freedom and selfhood in relation to one another. Western individualism, for all its benefits, has been in part a poisoned chalice.

3. The unique relation of Western civilization to science and technology scarcely needs comment. This, too, has been a double-edged gift to the world, and I shall have more to say about it in my comments later on environmental issues.

4. The self-critical spirit – the fourth of Roberts' list of European gifts to the world – has, of course, in part underlain the success of science. It has also stimulated Europe's capacity for change. It has removed old certainties. It creates strength

by self-correction, but it also undermines strength by sapping confidence. Indeed the question about moral values in Europe arises only because we have become so adept at debunking or relativizing any attempt to assert them.

This is not a complete description of Europe's gifts to the world, but it illustrates the difficulty of drawing any geographical boundary round the ideas and attitudes which have made Europe what it is. It can also indicate why so much of the non-Western world is trying so hard, and often so ineffectively, to dissociate itself from overt European influence while still retaining much of its heritage. And it provides an explanation for the pervasive feelings of European guilt, partly a fruit of the spirit of self-criticism, but also partly an acknowledgement of the extent to which our own failures have been exported to others.

This broad glance at our legacy can help to answer the narrower question about where the boundaries of the European Community should be drawn. It is a question fraught with political consequences. On the one hand, there are fears that too ready and rapid an expansion will jeopardize what the Community has already created, and frustrate the prospects of still closer integration. On the other hand, it is obvious both morally and politically that we cannot turn our backs on Eastern Europe and the former Soviet states, and that to do so will only feed already destructive enmities. Monnet's original vision seems once again to hold the clue. Given a sharing of interests, given some degree of participation in the Western European heritage, the boundaries should be drawn, not by the Community itself, but by those willing to accept the responsibilities and obligations its members have imposed upon themselves.

The nature of those obligations can be seen from what has happened to the former GDR, an example I have much in mind following a visit this week to Berlin. I remember many conversations in the days before 1989 with East German theologians who were determined to see positive value in their socialist state. Some of these are now under suspicion as collaborators, even though the ideals of close-knit democracy and alternative life style they were exploring were eventually subversive of the state. Their answer to repressive socialism was to set up alternative groups, radical, non-violent, committed to equality, drawing on the theology of the Sermon of the Mount to outdo socialism at its own game. And it was around these groups that the first public protests crystallized. Since 1989 the groups have virtually disappeared.

The so-called Round Table movement which spanned the period between the break-up of the communist government and the first elections, drew on the same Christian inspiration, and attempted a kind of government-by-consensus, in which all political groups were represented on a basis of equality. There was much talk of finding a third way between Socialism and Capitalism. It proved to be unworkable.

Following reunion the former Protestant Churches of East and West Germany have collaborated to produce a major report on economics. This was published in September 1991 under the title *Common Good and Self-Interest*. It is a powerful apologia for the social market economy as it has developed in West Germany, which claims already to enshrine the best principles of both socialism and capitalism. It roots itself theologically in a strong sense of responsibility for each other and for the environment. And it sees the future as more of the same, provided that it can develop better environmental policies, a more just functioning of the world economy, and can retain its democratic support.

The former GDR is relegated to an appendix to the report. This asks whether, without the challenge of a separate socialist GDR, the social factors of the social market economy are strong enough to allow their regulative powers on the market to take effect. Socialist utopianism has gone. The Christian utopianism which followed it barely touched the real problems. The report ends by noting the deep distrust felt by many East German Christians about whether the word 'social' in 'social market economy' carries any significant weight.

Two Czechoslovak theologians with whom I have been working this week have been asking themselves rather different questions. How is it possible to have a socially responsible society without the lie in the soul and the abuses of power which result from the attempt to impose a utopian vision?

All this, of course, is highly relevant to Maastricht's Social

Chapter. The Chapter is seen as the necessary counterpart to the market regulations, the safeguard against the degeneration of the Community into a mere economic arrangement. It is supposed to encapsulate some of the original moral and political vision. The fact that it is not seen in these terms by many in Britain is not a reason for ignoring the social side of the market economy.

It is impossible to do so, anyway. Nearly fifty per cent of the wealth generated by the Market goes into the public expenditure necessary to create the conditions in which the Market can flourish. How this expenditure is perceived, however, and how well it represents a moral vision of the kind of society we want, are key political questions which, Chapter or no Chapter, are answered by the way we conduct our public affairs. In Britain we seem fated to think of industrial investment and social investment as if they were in opposition to one another, rather than being mutually supportive. We are only just beginning to learn how to relate the interests of capital to the interests of wage earners, but it is still natural for us to think of taxation as a negative drag on business rather than to appreciate the social supports and infrastructures every business needs. It is therefore not surprising to find deep suspicions of European social policies, and I say this without making any prejudgement about whether in detail these are wise or foolish.

Britain is only one example of the ways in which culture and history complicate national interpretations of European obligations. The more we try to give content to those obligations, the more we become aware of diversity. If I am right in suggesting that the moral heart of Europe is to be found in the first instance in the acknowledgement of mutual obligations and responsibilities, with the examples of Germany and Britain in mind, we now have to ask whether it is possible to go further.

Is Europe so irrevocably pluralist, and so culturally divided, that it is foolish to hope for more than commitment to agreed working arrangements? Having accepted the Single Market, can we limit ourselves to practical directives for making it work, or are there values essential, not only for its efficiency but for its humanity? And if so, on what are they based? The question needs to be asked at several levels: at the level of social policy to which I have already referred; at the institutional level, not least in the values which undergird the business world; and at the personal level, in terms of the beliefs and values of ordinary citizens and the kind of constraints these impose on the democratic process.

The characteristics of European culture which I took from J. M. Roberts are not values in this sense, though they are elements which give Europe and its sphere of influence a certain coherence. In fact the critical, self-destructive strand in European culture reduces the chance of agreement on values. Pluralism seems inherent in the kind of people we are and the kind of civilization we have created for ourselves. But is it a pluralism with limits?

1. At the level of social policy the disagreements may be about ways and means, but they are at their sharpest, and most valuable, precisely when they are disagreements about values. One can see the truth of that in East Germany where the breakdown of the initial experiments in consensual politics were an important move away from one of the residual features of the monolithic state into the world of democratic politics. Consensus always has an attraction for Christian thinkers in our search for community. But it can suppresss real differences, give undue power to those who have an axe to grind, and paralyse decision-making by interminable debate. I frequently say to those who are shocked by differences of opinion in the Church of England on moral questions that this is the only way in which people can be honest in their search for the truth.

The debate between different value systems is essential to both political and moral life. There can, however, be agreement on procedures, and this is why one of the obligations laid on Community members is the possession of a democratic form of government. This in turn implies a respect for all citizens as having a place and voice in the conduct of their country's affairs, and many might go on to link this with the emphasis on the individual human being which Roberts saw as one of Europe's gifts to the world. Following on from this, it is easy to see how agreement on basic human rights also sets limits to pluralism.

The related issue of minority rights is much more difficult.

The legal and political problems of defining what counts as a minority and what corporate rights it might possess have generally led back to the affirmation of the rights of individuals within minorities, rather than to the rights of minorities as such. In a study in which I was involved a few years ago on *Human Rights and Responsibilities in Britain and Ireland* we saw a way forward through trying to devise political mechanisms for the protection of minorities which by-passed the tricky questions about precisely how a minority can be defined.

It is here that the notion of subsidiarity may help. I suspect most of us dislike the word, and are confused by it, but I feel a vested interest in retaining it as the only theological concept which has been widely accepted as part of the EC policy. The principle of subsidiarity affirms the right of people and groups to take decisions affecting themselves at the lowest appropriate level of organization. It is an affirmation of the local and the particular. I believe that if its implications were more fully worked out and if it were associated with a strong doctrine of personal rights and responsibilities, it might provide a sound moral basis for thinking constructively about minorities.

In this cluster of principles – the acceptance of mutual obligation and responsibilities, the balance between industrial and social investment, the commitment to human rights and to the principle of subsidiarity – I believe we can set limits to moral pluralism at the level of social and political policy. Christians, given a free hand, might want to say much more. But here is a possible bottom line.

2. At the institutional level, I referred to the values which undergird the business world. Not all controls on the market have to be at the level of government-inspired social legislation. There is already an elaborate system of conventions, assumptions and codes of conduct operating in the business world, and these need to be more clearly acknowledged as a vital factor in the moral basis of our European culture. In the last ten years or so there has been an impressive development in corporate codes of ethics, though Europe is still a long way behind the United States, and there are nagging suspicions as to how far many of them are mere window dressing.

Moves towards seeing companies as communities of people,

in which many others besides shareholders have an interest, may be another factor in helping to strengthen corporate culture, and so provide a firmer basis for ethics. Share-ownership schemes for employees are one example of the kind of thing I have in mind. It seems to me important, too, to strengthen the ethical bonds between companies, perhaps by the further development of business associations which can give some guarantee of the integrity of their members.

It will be obvious that I am no expert in this field. I mention it because it is frequently neglected in discussions of social ethics. The German report I mentioned earlier has been criticized on the grounds that the action sought in sustaining the social aspect of the social market economy was almost entirely at government level.

3. The third level at which questions need to be asked about the moral basis for our society is that of the individual. It is on this level that the politicians have expectations of the Churches, and the Churches themselves are most directly conscious of the prevailing pluralism.

From time to time I attend meetings of church leaders in Brussels to consider Community affairs, under the auspices of the European Ecumenical Commission for Church and Society. We meet under the shadow of the great European Commission building, conscious of being a very weak group, divided among ourselves, labelled ecumenical yet lacking Roman Catholic membership, and expected to give Christian advice on huge issues of European policy.

It is a tiny organization which has to live with the brute fact that institutionally few Churches within the European Community have much direct political influence. On the other hand, on the fringes of the Community and outside it, the role of different religious allegiances in nationalistic struggles is only too dreadfully obvious. This is not to say that the remaining Christian influence in Europe is unimportant or cannot be a force for good. But there is no way in which we can operate as if Christendom were still a reality. Christians must do their utmost to find unity among themselves and to strengthen Christian witness. Bodies like the EECCS, despite their weakness, can and do have a significant role in advising, alerting and correcting the bureaucrats, who are themselves sometimes more aware of their ideological nakedness than they are willing to admit in public. There is also the continuous task of the Churches in helping to create a climate of opinion within which politicians have a better chance of pursuing generous and far-sighted policies. But the background against which all this has to be done is, and for the foreseeable future will remain, pluralistic.

I am going to leave on one side the theological problems which pluralism creates for those who want to make absolute claims about their own proclamation of religious truth. I have tried to deal with these elsewhere. Instead I want to concentrate on the way in which religious bodies view themselves in a pluralist society.

One of the well-known consequences of pluralism is the privatization of belief. In the absence of public agreement about religious truth, religion becomes a matter for individuals. Beliefs become private opinions. And Churches become gatherings of the like-minded. Believers may, of course, not see their own faith in these terms, and may still assert its universal validity, but that is not what it looks like from the outside.

As a counter to this tendency there has been an attempt in recent years to look critically at so-called Western values from a specifically Christian perspective by a group called the Gospel and Culture movement. They trace back many of the ills of our present culture to the kind of assumptions which became popular during the Enlightenment. They propose a rebuilding of our intellectual heritage on explicitly Christian foundations, and urge Christians to seize what Bishop Hugh Montefiore has described as 'the moral high ground'.

I mention this movement because it has attracted a good deal of attention as an assertive, intellectually serious, and non-fundamentalist attempt to put Christianity back into the centre of our system of public values. However, while much of me sympathizes with this aim, I believe it has so far only succeeded in demonstrating that the high moral ground is not so easily captured. As I see it, many Christian values and insights are already embedded in our pluralist culture, and I believe the sound tactic is to try to identify these and reinforce them, rather than to dismantle the whole edifice and start again.

We need to dig down beneath apparent divisions to find common insights which, as a result of different historical developments, now manifest themselves in apparently incompatible forms. This has been the method pursued with enormous success among Christians within the ecumenical movement, and I believe there is scope for it too as between different religions and between religious and secular beliefs. To set out in this direction is not to deny the reality of differences. It is a refusal to allow ourselves to be shut up in our pluralist boxes as if there was no communication between them. It entails the conviction that to reduce such matters to the level of private opinion is to deny their very essence.

It is natural for me to say this as a member of the Church of England because the fundamental meaning of belonging to any established Church is that one is in some sense a guardian of public truth. This was expressed rather well in two brief sentences formulated a few years ago in discussions between the Church of England and the Church of Scotland on how we saw our responsibilities as national Churches in a pluralist and secular society. We saw them as, first, 'to hold in trust for the whole church and for all religious bodies the nation's religious commitment, i.e. its recognition of the place and importance of religion and religious freedom'; secondly, 'to discover a language in which the society may discuss itself in transcendental terms and agree on common values to inform its public ethics and policies'.

Here was a recognition that the acceptance of pluralism does not entail the abdication of responsibility. Without making imperialistic claims, it is possible for Churches to hold in trust the things for which they stand, and to make them available; to see themselves not simply as fighting for their own survival or aggrandizement but as servants for the whole community; to demonstrate between themselves the possibilities of unity in diversity; to keep alive a universal vision which transcends nationalism.

Parts of Europe have their own national Churches, though not quite in the helpfully haphazard way in which things were done in these islands. I am not suggesting that the rest of Europe should take its cue from the Church of England. But we have been learning in this country how to live with the anomaly of being nationally responsible without denying the reality of pluralism, and I believe part of our responsibility towards the rest of Europe is to share this experience. Pluralism may be a problem for those who want to issue a clear set of moral or doctrinal directives. It may also be a blessing in preserving us from the corruptions of too much power, and in allowing space for our God-given vitality to flourish in different ways. A pluralism in which there is also a seeking for common values, a pluralism in which there is also a sense of responsibility towards the whole, a pluralism set within the context of defined obligations, seems to me to provide the materials out of which Europe will rediscover its soul.

The kind of moral vision which emerges is going to be tested by the three major issues confronting the European Community at the moment. I end with no more than a mention of these, because each deserves a lecture of its own.

I mentioned earlier the role of science and technology in creating environmental problems. This is one of our European exports. To be fair, scientists and technologists have also had a role in alerting us to the problems, and sometimes in alleviating them. There is no point in trying to assign blame for the environmental dangers we now face. But it is essential to accept responsibility, and that is why the kind of lead given by the European Market in its environmental policies is going to be so crucially important for the world. Rio will be as much a test of European intentions as Copenhagen.

The second major issue concerns the treatment of minorities. It is an offshoot of the discussion on pluralism, and there is no need for me to emphasize its relevance in the wider European scene with the present resurgence of nationalisms. In the European Community there are the problems of migrants, and difficult decisions in the near future on policies towards asylum. But perhaps the major issue in the long-term future concerns the place of Islam within Europe.

There was a time when Europe defined itself over against Islam. There are tendencies in parts of Islam today to define itself over against Europe. There are the inherent difficulties within Islam itself in discovering how to be true to itself within a pluralist society. There is the attraction of Islam with its certainties and its strong social solidarity for those emerging from recent communist rule. I have no solutions to offer. It is just possible that in Britain, where our experience of

Islam is rather different from that on the Continent, we may have a contribution to make if we can handle our affairs well. Meanwhile I simply note it as an issue.

The third, and perhaps greatest, moral challenge facing Europe concerns its relationship with the rest of the world, and particularly the developing and undeveloped world. The point is constantly being made, and I have no need to elaborate it. The only question I want to ask is, where in the moral vision I have tried to articulate do we find the moral imperative to care for the world's poor? I have spoken about mutual obligations and responsibilities, but these are obligations which nations accept freely for themselves and for their mutual benefit. I have spoken about human rights, and there is obvious leverage in these in trying to secure international economic arrangements in which nations can compete on a basis of equality, since all share an equal dignity as human beings. I have spoken about ethically based business arrangements, and about how to make a responsible Christian contribution within a pluralist society.

But I believe any effective acknowledgement that we cannot be merely Europeans, that we are one world, that we are responsible for one another, and that we need one another, has to be rooted in something more profound and demanding. It is no coincidence that it is precisely here that the Christian voice is heard most loudly. We must love one another because we are commanded to do so. We must love one another because that is the condition for our existence. We can love one another, because what God commands, he gives us the grace to fulfil.

11

The Role of the Churches in the International Order

The Thomas Corbishley Lecture, delivered at Heythrop College, London, 9 October 1991

I can recall a conversation some ten years ago with a Russian theologian about the USSR's failure to make any meaningful response to the revolution in Iran. He described how foreign policy had been paralysed because there was no place for any such event in Marxist–Leninist theory. Nor was it only Marxist theoreticians who were taken by surprise. In 1979 religion stepped onto the international stage in a way which confounded social and political analysts of every hue. And it has continued to do so.

The ten years which followed have seen the breakdown of standard sociological theories about the progressive marginalization of religion – its retreat from public life to private life. It is now clear that modernization does not, as was once supposed, lead inexorably to secularization. The main impetus behind Islamic fundamentalism has arisen not from an ignorant peasantry, but for the most part from those who are young, upward moving and scientifically or technologically educated. And it is not only in the Middle East that the religious dimension in politics is impossible to ignore. The religiousness of America is not an inexplicable and fading aberration, but seems to be a central element in national self-

123

understanding. The revolutions of 1989 and onwards, though not inspired directly by religion, have almost invariably included religious factors. Indeed the transformation in Poland can be seen as starting ten years earlier with the first visit by the Pope. The East German and Romanian revolutions began in Churches. Lutherans in East Germany had developed a theological critique of communism which made them natural leaders when the decisive moment came. In Romania the situation was much more complex because the Orthodox Church had for the most part become subservient to the regime: it was a Protestant pastor who sparked off the revolt. In the USSR the role of religion has been full of ironies. I was part of a meeting of church leaders in Moscow in July of 1989. We were addressed in one of the great halls in the Kremlin by the then Prime Minister, Nikolai Ryzhkov, who spoke about the great importance of the Churches in providing a moral and humanitarian basis for society in a time of transition. The Russian Orthodox Church now faces a daunting, and perhaps impossible task, in trying to fill a huge ideological vacuum. In South Africa, I believe, the main hope for a stable future lies in the willingness of the Churches to work together. And in Zaire the Churches seem to be the only credible institutions left.

Perceptions about the role of religion in the modern world have indeed been changing. Further symptoms of the change are to be found in the cluster of feelings and shifts of attitude associated with post-modernism, environmentalism, the re-actions against the dominance of economics and bureaucratiz-ation, the search for 'soul'. The European Community in recent months has deliberately been opening doors to the Churches as allies in broadening its concerns beyond the market to the underlying values and social provisions needed to undergird it.

In a word, the role of the Churches in the international order is now in the melting-pot. The Churches in many parts of the world are faced with dramatic new opportunities and dramatic demands on their resources. The fact that we here in Britain tend to be locked all too frequently in stale old domestic controversies should not blind us to what is happening elsewhere.

The Roman Catholic Church has, of course, always been

consciously international. Its possession of the Papal States has given it an entrée into international politics, which other Churches have never possessed, and not really wanted. Nevertheless I think it is true to say that its first steps in tackling some of the modern questions raised by a changing international order were taken at just about the same time as other Churches were feeling their way towards the same kind of issues. I have in mind the Papal Encyclical of 1891 on the new understandings of society and the state, and its splendid sequel, *Centesimus Annus*, promulgated by Pope John Paul II earlier this year. There is an alternative lecture which ought to be given on that tradition – perhaps a more appropriate one than this, in view of our wish to honour Thomas Corbishley. But in what follows I am going to concentrate on a different tradition, the development of social and international thinking in the World Council of Churches. And I do so because that is where for the past twelve years my own involvement has been.

Churches cannot be true to their message if they ignore the international dimension. Christianity, like Islam, is a missionary faith, and both faiths, unlike Judaism, have seen the world as their parish. In fact the decisive break between Christianity and Judaism was on precisely this issue, whether the faith was potentially universal or whether it was the faith of a chosen people of limited extent. It is also regrettably true that Christian Churches have frequently lost their universal vision and been captured by various nationalisms – and still are in many parts of the world. But it is rare to find a Christian Church these days which does not have some inkling that it belongs to something wider, something supra-national, something, in the broadest sense of the word, ecumenical. In the past hundred years that wider dimension has increasingly been represented, not just through missionary endeavour, but through a concern for the well-being of the world as a whole. The growth of international aid, the more modern interest in world development and international justice, the long-standing concern for peace and the humane conduct of war, and the huge network of contacts and cross-linkages which now exist between Churches in every part of the world, all these are evidence in their different ways that the international dimension of church life is taken seriously. And all of them, at least in the non-Roman Catholic Churches, have been linked more or less closely with the growth of the ecumenical movement, which itself developed out of an awareness of the implications of world mission.

All Churches, however, face similar dilemmas in tackling social and political questions because all are aware of the religious ambivalence of political power. In all our traditions there are terrible examples of the abuse of power, and of the dire effects of too close a linkage between political and religious interests. Difficult political problems, as in the Middle East or Ireland, become virtually insoluble if religious affiliations and alignments are invoked in support of political differences. Some of the present divisions in Yugoslavia and other Balkan states have a potentially dangerous religious dimension to them. And who needs reminding of the sad record through history of the religious persecution of minorities?

Yet it can be equally dangerous to withdraw from political concern when the only effective voice against injustice, or tyranny, or narrow nationalism can come from a body which claims to speak in the name of a higher authority. And it is not just in such extreme negative contexts that religious realities have political implications. Political life, and especially democratic politics, needs a secure basis in moral values, and morals without roots in a structured system of beliefs can become perilously fragile. It is not surprising when, in a democracy, politicians look to Churches for moral legitimation, and it is not unreasonable for Churches to try to provide it. But cautiously. And always conscious of a fundamental Christian dualism between God and Caesar, between being in the world yet not being captured by the world.

It is the tensions in this dualism which have shaped the changing involvement of the ecumenical movement in some of the international issues of this century, and which provide the basis for the story I now want to tell.

In the latter part of the nineteenth century and the early years of this, the idea of an international order which the Churches could play their part in creating and maintaining, fitted well the picture of an expanding Church gradually spreading its civilizing influence over the globe. Colonial law and order went hand in hand with missionary enterprise, and the disaster of the First World War only strengthened the case for effective instruments to administer such law world-wide. Much ecumenical effort was put into building up 'the brotherhood of man' under 'the fatherhood of God', and the Churches were active in a whole series of conferences and campaigns in the interests of peace and friendship and mutual understanding, and the development of international law, the League of Nations, and ultimately the United Nations.

This work still continues. Right at the beginning of its life in 1946 the WCC took the decision to establish a Commission of the Churches on International Affairs, and this has always seen a major part of its task as relating to the UN as an officially recognized consultative body, as well as relating to many non-governmental organizations. One of the Commission's first tasks was to participate actively in the drafting of the Universal Declaration of Human Rights. Since then it has worked consistently for the implementation and development of such rights. Though it has never been shy of criticizing particular political regimes, its main thrust has always been to work with the powers-that-be in the interests of stabilizing and strengthening an albeit imperfect world order.

Undergirding this vision of world order has been the belief that the unity of the Church is, or ought to be, in some sense a microcosm of the unity of humanity. Ecumenism, in other words, is not merely a churchy thing, still less a bureaucratic exercise in ecclesiastical joinery. The patient building of international trust, and of instruments to embody that trust, is part and parcel of the same impulse which leads Christians to look for their unity in Christ. Thus the WCC has tried to hold the two tasks together, and the phrase 'The Unity of the Church and the Unity of Humankind' was explicitly part of its agenda from 1971 to 1981. Since 1981 there has been a greater willingness to recognize that other faiths are not going to go away, and that the world is irreducibly pluralist. It has become obvious that the notion of international order is much more complex than it once seemed, but a striving for order has remained an important part of the Churches' task.

Alongside this concern there developed a strong ecumenical tradition of constructive social criticism, particularly in the period from about 1930 to about 1970. The impotence of the League of Nations, economic collapse, the huge suffering of the Second World War, and the social disruption which followed it, were the background against which innumerable church conferences tried to articulate some vision of a less disordered world imbued by sanity, fairness and security. One of the fruits of all this thought was the idea of the 'Responsible Society', and this dominated ecumenical thinking on social matters for some twenty or thirty years. The Responsible Society was defined by the first Assembly of the WCC in 1948 as 'one where freedom is the freedom of men who acknowledge responsibility to justice and public order, and where those who hold political authority or economic power are responsible for its exercise to God and the people whose welfare is affected by it'.

In other words the ideal was a free democratic society, resting on a shared moral basis, whether Christian or not, in which people accepted responsibility for themselves and for each other under constraints which transcended particular political or economic systems. This may now seem rather platitudinous, but in the world of the 1940s it was nothing of the kind. Nor a dozen years later was it to sound platitudinous as an ideal for developing countries beginning to discover the implications of self-determination.

What eventually pushed it off the ecumenical agenda had more to do with method than content, and it is worth pausing for a moment to spell out what that method was.

It had been introduced into the ecumenical movement by J. H. Oldham, one of the two main lay architects of the movement, in the early 1930s. His method was to seek out lay experts who, he believed, could best help the Churches understand the social and political crises of the day. These were usually inveigled into the job by lunches at the Athenaeum. With the help of these experts the main themes were teased out, and formed the agenda for prolonged interdisciplinary dialogue between expert groups of laity and theologians. Reports were then offered to the Churches for study and action. Though a familiar method in all sorts of contexts nowadays, it was something of an innovation then, and it produced some quite impressive results. Many people of real calibre who wanted to look deeper into the moral and spiritual implications of their own expertise were attracted into such groups, and a generation of theologians was forced to look at problems which it had hitherto ignored, and to respect, and learn from the expertise placed at its disposal. I myself had the good fortune to attend the last great conference at which some of the fruits of this method were brought together, though by then, for reasons which we shall see, it was already on the verge of collapse. This was the 1979 World Conference on Science, Faith and the Future, held in the Massachusetts Institute of Technology. The Conference brought together an astonishing array of some nine hundred scientists, technologists, theologians, church leaders, industrialists and politicians from every part of the world. It nearly collapsed because the method and the assumptions underlying it were no longer universally acceptable. In fact the most dramatic moment in the Conference came when a group of scientists from Africa, Asia, Latin America, the Middle East and the Pacific denounced the supposed objectivity of what they called 'Western' science and technology, and urged 'the scientists of the world to accept as the sole purpose of their work the alleviation of misery of the poor and oppressed'.

What had happened in the intervening period, between the heyday of the Oldham method and such radical denunciation in 1979, was a massive change both in the composition of the WCC and in its agenda. From the early 1960s onwards third world issues and perspectives began to predominate. The Oldham method was viewed with suspicion as élitist, abstract, Western in style and orientation, and lacking the revolutionary potential which radicalized Christians were more and more reading into the gospel. There was increasing emphasis on widespread participation in every process of decision-making, with particular attention paid to hitherto poorly represented groups, women, youth, black, third world, poor, disabled, and latterly, so-called indigenous peoples – Aborigines and native Americans. Prophetic witness from situations of dire poverty or oppression began to take precedence over careful social and political analysis. What had formerly been a global concern with international order and the structures needed to maintain it, turned towards a more localized series of issues within states, and not merely between them. The role of liberation movements and the rights of minorities have occupied much recent ecumenical attention. The sense of powerlessness experienced in economically weak countries in the face of transnational corporations has been a constant source of complaint – whether justifiably or not. Questions about the location of power, and particularly about the consequences of militarism in unstable or oppressive regimes, have seemed more urgent and important than supposedly abstract questions about social or international order.

I have done no more than list a few of the shifts of perspective in this second stage of the WCC's history. It is possible to mark the transitions by seeing what happened to the concept of the Responsible Society. In 1978 this was abandoned in favour of a new slogan – the Just, Participatory and Sustainable Society. It was not everybody's idea of a snappy title, but the notion of being responsible no longer seemed adequate to those whose experiences had been shaped by poverty, oppression, racism, the traumas of decolonization, and above all by the need to be involved in assessing the purposes behind development programmes, and their likely effects. The 1978 Assembly, meeting in Nairobi, defined development as 'essentially a people's struggle in which the poor and the oppressed should be the active agents and immediate beneficiaries'. Hence 'just and participatory'. 'Sustainable' was a new concept, and a useful one, a first recognition of environmental issues, echoing the subsequently much criticized report by the Club of Rome on Limits to Growth.

Unfortunately 'sustainability' proved to be the Achilles' heel of this particular slogan. Church representatives from developing nations were less than enthusiastic about committing themselves to limits merely because the affluent West was beginning to feel guilty and threatened by its own extravagance. 'A sustainable society' began to look uncomfortably like one in which poor nations were trapped even more irrevocably in their poverty.

The idea of 'participation' created some problems too. It is one of the tragedies of the WCC that in trying to escape from its old élitism through its commitment to wide participation, it has also managed to lose much of its expertise. I shall return to this theme a little later.

'Justice', the third ingredient of this slogan, is, as we all know, easy to aspire to, and hard to define. It alone survived in the new slogan, born in 1983, and now the main focus of much of the WCC's current work. 'Justice, Peace and the Integrity of Creation' is vaguer than its predecessor. Its main merit is that it links together social, international and environmental issues which in ordinary political life have frequently been kept apart, though perhaps less so nowadays. The burning oilfields of Kuwait symbolize effectively the environmental implications of war. The threat to the rain forests in Central America has to be understood in the context of gross social inequalities and grinding poverty, both of which have international as well as national dimensions. Examples are legion. As a focus for a multitude of practical concerns, and as a warning against one-sidedness, the slogan has some inspirational value. But as a guide to policy-making, it has proved virtually useless because its terms are too large and ill-defined. Justice and peace are as easily commendable as motherhood and apple pie, whereas the phrase 'integrity of creation' has defied all exegesis. A world conference on the theme in Seoul in 1990 produced only an incoherent hotchpotch of well-intentioned exhortations. And the WCC Assembly in Canberra earlier this year fared not much better.

I tell this sad story of decline in precision and effectiveness without in any way wishing to be cynical. The Churches have genuinely tried to listen to the cries of anger and suffering in so many parts of the world, and have done it rather well. One of the great present strengths of the WCC is that it can act as a sounding board on a world stage for those whose political plight, or sense of injustice, or warnings about disaster, might otherwise never be heard. It is immensely valued by Christians in countries where Churches are tiny minorities, by those living under oppressive regimes, and by those who feel their political powerlessness. It matters hugely to them that their problems can be voiced and that they can feel under protection from a world Christian body. Powerful resolutions about the world's trouble spots can be surprisingly important to those who live in the middle of the trouble. And those of us who live in more comfortable circumstances can learn a good deal about ourselves in a world forum where such issues are aired by people who are not afraid to say what they think.

There is a strongly positive side, therefore, to the changes which have overtaken the WCC in the last thirty years. But there has also been a disastrous loss of credibility, particularly in the realm of social, economic and political policy. This has made the Churches much less effective on the international scene than one might have expected at a time when religion is once again coming centre stage. To see why, I want to explore two related reasons, first by returning to the theme of participation, and secondly by illustrating the effects of loss of expertise.

Participation is in one sense what world Christianity is all about. We are members one of another. Human life has a God-given dignity and worth such that everybody matters, and everybody's contribution to the building of true human community under God is needed. There may be various ways of enabling people to participate in this process, but there should be no doubts about our goal. Nor is there any doubt that bodies like the WCC, which have taken such participation seriously, have raised the self-consciousness and morale of many people who would not otherwise have thought of themselves as in any sense Christian decision-makers.

The so-called 'preferential option for the poor', now an official part of Roman Catholic teaching as well as a keynote in WCC thinking, points in the same direction. It is not just about righting economic imbalances but about empowering the marginalized. It has deep roots in Christian theology, not just in the many biblical references to God's concern for the poor, but in the central event of Christianity itself. On the cross God is revealed in weakness, identified with outcasts, and manifests his true nature, not in an exhibition of power, but in the acceptance of suffering. 'He saved others. Himself he could not save.' And so, if this is God, this God made poor for the sake of a disordered world, our own efforts at rebuilding this world have to begin precisely where God is – among the poorest.

That in a nutshell is what I think the preferential option for the poor is about. It is a theological insight, not a reflection of economic envy. And it makes the valid point that if we want to understand the true character of a society we need to look at it from below, at the point where the shoe pinches, or even where there is no shoe to pinch. Participatory programmes which entail giving prominence to that kind of perspective are surely part of Christian witness to the nature of God and the unity of mankind.

But what do we do with this perspective from below? Do we allow it simply to dictate our decisions? Or do we incorporate it into all our thinking as a vital element in a more complex process of decision-making? Is a preferential option for the poor a preferential option simply to endorse and adopt the declared wishes of the poor, or rather to take due account of their needs and the validity of their experiences?

The treatment given to Aboriginal people at the Canberra Assembly of the WCC last February is a good illustration of the dilemma. Much attention was rightly given at the Assembly to the shameful treatment of the Aborigines during the colonial era, and their present marginalization within Australian society. They were given a prominent place in the Assembly worship and in its programme. The Churches made a strenuous effort to hear them, to accept their anger and look for ways of redress. But such is the emotional pressure built up where sympathetic listening feeds into the stream of innumerable other discontents and guilt feelings, that it becomes hard to say No to manifest nonsense.

In preparation for the Assembly Aboriginal leaders had drawn up their own statement setting out their hopes of improving their status, and within this the idea of Aboriginal sovereignty had come to have high symbolic value. It became a kind of focus for aspirations about a fair deal in compensation for loss of land. Nobody seems to have imagined setting up an Aboriginal state. But the use of the word 'sovereignty' as seen from below carries very different connotations when set out in a resolution by the world's Churches. The Churches, for example, were called upon 'to recognise, acknowledge and vigorously support self-determination and sovereignty of indigenous people, as defined by them, in church and society'.

Elsewhere the Assembly said: 'We recognize that indigenous peoples of Australia were independent, self-governing peoples long before Europeans invaded their land, and that they have a right to regain such control over their land under their own rule.' Some resolution! But of course nobody meant it in any straightforward sense. They meant to express sympathy and solidarity, but what they actually said was absurd. The only effect of it could be to reduce the credibility of those who said it. What is missing from all this, as it has been missing, alas, from so much recent work emanating from the WCC, is the broad critical understanding of a complex subject, which is precisely what the old élitism used to provide. Unless the voices of the poor are somehow taken up into a larger frame of reference, those who stand in solidarity with them will themselves cease to be heard.

This brings me to my second reason for fearing that the new prominence religion has acquired in world affairs is not going to be used effectively – the loss of expertise.

The need for expertise in economics, for example, has become urgent in the search for some third way between socialism and capitalism in Eastern Europe. The Churches there have looked for guidance to the Churches of the West, which are themselves in disarray because so much ecumenical thought on economic issues has been tied to socialist models. Development and the needs of the third world have been the keynote. In 1967 Pope Paul VI went so far as to state, 'Development is the new name of peace'. More recently the role of transnational corporations in developing countries, and the laissez-faire image of capitalism derived from Latin America and the experience of third world debt, have set the scene for economic discussion. Economists who might have given a more favourable view of democratic capitalism have simply not been heard. The main aspiration has been for what was called 'A New Economic Order', and its heavily interventionist character has not really been questioned. Property has been seen primarily in terms of power, and little attention has been paid to its relation with freedom and democracy.

A recent essay by an Indian economist, a key figure in the WCC's economic thinking, tries to respond to the events since 1989, and is properly critical of centralized command economies. Nevertheless when the author goes on to lay down some general principles for the future, he includes these: the alternative system 'must institutionalize the responsibility to decide what will be produced, how much will be produced, and how production forces will be put to use to meet today's needs and the needs of the future. In thus submitting economic processes to conscious social decision it must ensure that its decision-making arrangements are genuinely democratic and participatory.'

Isn't this where we came in?

The Canberra Assembly had no specific advice to offer

Eastern Europe, but it said this about economics in general:

> The vast and shameful arms trade illustrates clearly the immorality of our world economic order; it is one of the root causes of the Gulf War. The international ecumenical movement has for years criticized the lack of economic democracy, social injustice, and the stimulation of human greed. But flagrant international inequality in the distribution of income, knowledge, power and wealth persists. Acquisitive materialism has become the dominant ideology of our day. The irresponsible exploitation of the created world continues. Changes will only come by active opposition and informed and responsible social pressure.

Pressure to do what? It would be unfair to criticize an inspirational statement of this kind if there was some solid thinking which lay behind it. But the people capable of doing this thinking and coming to a realistic assessment of what is practically possible, are no longer there.

As I said at the beginning, I have been telling a sad story, a story partly in self-criticism because I have myself been heavily involved in the WCC, and believe in its importance despite its obvious shortcomings. It has fumbled badly in a world which has been changing out of all recognition. I could have spoken about other failures, in particular its failure to make a credible response to the Gulf War which took place while the Canberra Assembly was meeting. In fact it was only the British who had the temerity to maintain in public that Iraq's invasion of Kuwait could not be allowed by the international community to stand, and that there might actually be good reasons for resisting aggression – by force if necessary. But they carried no conviction. Anti-colonialism, anti-militarism, anti-Americanism, an instinct to side with the underdog, and above all a lack of consistent theological thinking about the conditions under which war might justifiably be waged, made it impossible for the arguments in favour to be received. But even so it is important that they were stated and heard.

Nevertheless, despite its failures and its incompetences, the existence of a world Christian forum dedicated to wrestling with the world's problems is a sign of hope. I have criticized it for twelve years because I want it to be better. But I have been committed to it for twelve years because a Christianity which paid no attention to global issues, and was unwilling to learn, however uncomfortably, from different world perspectives, would be faithless to its calling. The WCC tries to do this, and my hope is that as its members work through the stage of anger and frustration at the manifest injustices of our present world, they may begin to see once again the need for careful, balanced, professionally informed analysis. They need to bridge the gulf between prophetic denunciation and sensible policy-making. And I hope they may gain some encouragement to do this from those who are themselves involved in world affairs and who believe in the need for a credible Christian voice, able to command attention and respect.

I suspect that the present resurgence of religion in many cultures around the world is not just a blip in the chart. It represents a deeply important element in being human, because the essence of our humanity, as I see it, is the drive towards self-transcendence. However inept, therefore, the attempts of the Churches to respond to the hugely complex social and political demands of our times, they still have something of inestimable value to offer in setting them in a larger context. World-embracing Christian concern and the wide variety of world Christian experience provide part of that context. But the level on which each person has to come to terms with God and with their own selves, is another part of it. That is why I am going to end this lecture with a quotation from perhaps the most perceptive Christian commentator on the world scene this century – Reinhold Niebuhr.

Nothing worth doing is completed in our lifetime; therefore we must be saved by hope. Nothing true or beautiful or good makes complete sense in any immediate context of history; therefore we must be saved by faith. Nothing we do, however virtuous, can be accomplished alone; therefore we are saved by love. No virtuous act is quite as virtuous from the standpoint of our friend or foe as from our own standpoint. Therefore we must be saved by the final form of love, which is forgiveness.

12

Church and State

The Price Waterhouse Lecture, delivered at the London School of Economics, 25 October 1989

One of my predecessors was tried for his life in the year 1405 in what is now our dining-room and was executed the same day. His crime was to find himself on the wrong side in the Wars of the Roses. The picture of him which still hangs in the room is a constant reminder that relations between Church and state may have a certain cutting edge of danger.

That, however, is only one possible relationship. The variety is enormous, and my intention is to look very broadly at a number of them, drawing first on some familiar biblical material, then describing forms of interaction between religion and politics from a political perspective, and finally trying to draw some lessons for the relation between Church and state in England today.

Every politician nowadays can quote the words, 'Render to Caesar the things that are Caesar's and to God the things that are God's.' They are commonly taken as describing a useful division of powers, leaving the politician to get on with politics, and the religious to get on with religion, without mutual interference. But that conveniently ignores the fact that the cleverest part of Jesus' answer to the question, 'Is it lawful to pay tribute to Caesar or not?' lay in his request,

'Show me a penny'. His questioners' ability to produce one was evidence that they were already involved in Caesar's world. The tribute money was a special coinage, one of the outward signs of Roman sovereignty. Their possession of it was thus an admission of that sovereignty and a sign that they, like all of us, were inevitably mixed up in it and compromised by it. Of course we have to render to Caesar the things that are his because, like it or not, we are part of Caesar's world.

It is only when this is understood that the punchline becomes significant, 'Render to God the things that are God's.' And that means *everything*, even the things which appear to be Caesar's. Thus the inevitability of political compromise does not remove or reduce our overriding duty to God.

This theme is given a different twist in Romans 13, where under the famous rubric 'The powers that be are ordained of God', St Paul sets out his view of the authority of the secular power, notwithstanding that the secular power was Nero. The point seems to be that even a bad state can provide a context in which good people can flourish, and that almost anything is better than anarchy.

The danger of this interpretation, which has had a long Christian history, is that it can induce an attitude of submissiveness towards the state, and an acceptance of the status quo in situations where anarchy is not a real danger. It disarms those who see the risk of anarchy as preferable to continued injustice and tyranny. In Christian theories of the state which have taken the text at its face value, notably in Luther's Two Kingdom theology, a useful distinction has been drawn between motivation and political necessity. The motivation of a Christian ought to be the inner liberty of a person set free by Christ. Such freedom has no direct application, however, in the realm of political necessity which is governed by its own laws and inner dynamic. Nevertheless, political necessity is best served by people who have been set free from self-preoccupation, in other words by those who according to the theory are Christianly motivated. There is obvious truth in this. Democracy will only work if enough people have high enough moral standards, and if at least some people can rise fairly consistently above self-concern.

But the distinction between religious motivation and political necessity also carries great dangers, as was evident during the German church crisis under Hitler. If the state's authority under God is unchallengeable or if, as happened to some theologians, a sense of historical destiny is interpreted as being the mind of God, the result can be political and moral disaster.

A totally opposite view of the relation between Church and state underlies the whole of the Book of Revelation. Here the state is presented as Antichrist, the great whore, Babylon ripe for destruction. The tone is apocalyptic. The context is that of a church undergoing persecution. And the result is a different kind of otherworldliness, not this time the otherworldliness of those who recognize that the state has a proper autonomy, but the otherworldliness of those who withdraw from the state, or society, or from unbelievers in general, confident that in due time God will vindicate and save his elect, whether in this world or the next.

A rejection of the state as Antichrist can also give rise to a more active Christian response, namely the attempt to subvert it. The group of theologians who produced the so-called Kairos document in South Africa argue along these lines. In a state which has forfeited its moral authority, as they interpret it, by acts of oppression and by systematic injustice, the proper Christian response is subversion or rebellion. Yet another variation on the apocalyptic style of interpreting relations between Church and state, was the curious period in the recent history of the United States when there were real fears that its foreign policy might be guided, under strong fundamentalist pressure, by the prophecies of Daniel and Ezekiel.

The New Testament's most profound symbol of the tangled and ambivalent relationship between Church and state is to be found in the story of Jesus before Pontius Pilate, in John chapters 18 and 19. Seen from one angle, these present a picture of Jesus as rising above, and indifferent to, the machinations of secular power and secularized religious authority, by claiming that his Kingdom is 'not of this world'. Yet it is this very world which, according to St John, he has come to save. Its need for salvation is nowhere more apparent than when God's own people are driven into a corner by Pilate, and reject the very assertion of God's sovereignty on which their special calling rests. 'We have no king but Caesar.'

Yet Pilate, despite his subtlety, is himself shown to be impotent and driven by fear. The civil power, in other words, is not so much evil as ineffective, caught in the insoluble conflict created by what it perceives as religious fanaticism.

It's possible to have some sympathy with Pilate at a time when the most intractable conflicts in today's world are fuelled by a deadly mixture of religion and politics. In the face of such dilemmas it is all the more important for Christians to take seriously Jesus' assertion that his true power lay out of this world, yet also to be aware of how, nevertheless, he was ineluctably involved in the world as the one who bore its evil and suffering. These chapters sublimely reveal the tragedy of power. Perhaps we can find within them some understanding of why it never corrupts more disastrously than when it is used in the service of idealism.

I take my final comment in this very brief survey from the Epistle to Diognetus. This was probably written in the third century, and reveals something of Christian self-understanding in the period when the Church was still a persecuted minority but was much more ready to see a role for itself in the world of its day.

> What the soul is in the body, that Christians are in the world. The soul is dispersed through all the members of the body, and Christians are scattered through all the cities of the world. The soul dwells in the body, but does not belong to the body, and Christians dwell in the world but do not belong to the world. The soul, which is invisible, is kept under guard in the visible body; in the same way, Christians are recognized when they are in the world, but their religion remains unseen . . .

There are echoes here of the New Testament parables of the salt and the yeast, which pervade the materials in which they reside, and bring taste and substance to them while working secretly. They can serve as reminders of the hugely important theme of the Kingdom of God, and the relation between Church and Kingdom, which has provided the focus for much present-day Christian thinking on the topic of this lecture.

The great change occurred, of course, when the Church, far from being an almost invisible minority, found itself with spiritual responsibility for the crumbling Roman Empire. In one sense the scriptural story ends here and a new story begins, but in working out that new story Christians have constantly gone back to the kind of materials I have briefly described. The main thing to be said about them in summary is that they are highly diverse. There is no one model to which Church and state should conform, and the history of relations between Churches and the civil power demonstrates how that diversity has been fully explored. Nevertheless it is possible to identify a kind of middle ground in which recognition is given to two distinct realms, the religious and the political, as each possessing its own integrity, while at the same time each needs the other, and can live in different kinds of constructive tension with it in different ages and settings. This is a reason for approaching the question of Church and state in England, when we come to it, to a large extent pragmatically, rather than on the basis of some fixed theoretical understanding of what an ideal relationship between Church and state should be. The long history of Christian thought and experience in these matters must clearly inform us, but it cannot provide definitive answers.

I turn now to the other side of this equation, the political perspective, which I propose to analyse in terms of the balance between three factors: critical rationality, mythology and practical necessity. These are set out in classic form in the life and death of Socrates.

Critical rationality is represented by the rule of the philosopher kings. This is government by the wise and knowledgeable élite who, in terms of Plato's analogy of the cave, have been able to glimpse reality beyond the play of shadows on the wall, which is all most men see. Here we have the Socratic ideal of enlightenment through rational argument and criticism.

It stands in sharp contrast to the squalid diplomacy practised in the Athenian state in Socrates' day. Expediency ruled, and was held at least in international affairs to justify treachery and murder. The abstract excellence of which Socrates dreamt counted as nothing against the need for practical effectiveness.

Despite this, those who ruled by expediency remained well aware of its limits. Socrates was tried and executed, not for dreaming of an ideal state, but for 'corrupting the youth' by undermining the myths on which the cohesion of the state

141

depended. It is possible to pay tribute to reason, even while ruling with naked power, but states are not in practice held together for long by either of them. Mythology in its broadest sense is the necessary third element in the triad, and Socrates died because his critical rationality threatened to destroy it.

These three elements, all present in these seminal attempts to theorize about politics, can form useful co-ordinates for mapping different kinds of political thinking. What I hope briefly to demonstrate is that the relation between religion and politics in different ages and settings depends on the balance between the co-ordinates; and as a corollary, that exclusive concentration on any one of them leads to tyranny.

I begin with the religous/mythological co-ordinate which, in its exclusive form, is theocracy. Islamic fundamentalism is the most obvious example of this religious exclusivism in today's world, and is rooted in the search for a radical alternative to what are perceived as Western power politics and secular rationalism. Its potential for tyranny does not need to be spelt out. Fundamentalism in the United States is altogether less formidable, and seems to have moved into the public realm more as a result of the moral vacuum there than through strong political impetus. Unlike its Islamic counterpart it tends to be caught in an internal paradox. In a pluralist culture such as that of the United States an authoritarian faith which is not open to rational argument finds itself treated willy-nilly as a private faith, no matter what public claims it may be making. This inevitably weakens its impact. Nevertheless in localized settings it too has its potential for tyranny.

Strongly held political ideologies count on this analysis as secular versions of the attempt to establish theocracy. One part of the critical rational task, not least in our own day, is to expose such ideological commitments for what they are, and to signal the points at which political policies have ceased to be either rational or pragmatic and have become doctrinaire.

These are all examples of extreme uses of mythology. In more normal circumstances the religious/mythological co-ordinate makes itself felt in a variety of important ways.

Private morality is the most basic of these, and I have already made the point that democracy depends upon there being a sufficiency of good people to work it. Such basic private morality is in some respects worryingly depleted in

Britain today, and the Churches have been taken to task for their failure to nourish it – a failure for which they must share part of the blame. Churches are not immune from the intellectual and moral revolutions of our time and it is obvious that there is great and continuing confusion in some aspects of private morality.

However, it also needs to be said that private morality lacks strength and consistency if it is cut off from its roots in community faith. Individual standards are essential, but they actually grow and are sustained in the atmosphere created by public standards, and there are not many people who can persevere indefinitely with their own vision without community support. This is why the 'privatization of faith', for all its resonances of sturdy individualism, proves in the long run to be a weakness rather than a strength. The refusal of the Churches to concern themselves simply with individuals rests on this perception, and the kind of question they have consistently tried to force back on politicians is, What kind of societies produce what kind of people?

The question points directly to a second main way in which the religious/mythological co-ordinate makes its presence felt, namely through culture and tradition. Broadly what is meant by these in this context is the accumulation of a common pool of values, rules and beliefs, whether religious or secular, which act as a counterbalance to individual self-interest.

Rousseau saw this very clearly and was aware of the dilemma posed by earlier Enlightenment thinking as it tried to grapple with ethical and political questions on the basis of what is 'natural' to human beings. Such an approach can never overcome the pull of self-interest because self-interest is in itself most deeply 'natural'. There therefore needs to be created a set of assumptions and constraints which will enable people to feel and know that they belong to a larger whole, in other words, to a political culture. The legislator according to Rousseau must 'so to speak change human nature, transform each individual who by himself is a perfect and solitary whole, into a part of a greater whole from which that individual as it were gets his life and his being'.

In the Enlightenment tradition this transformation of the 'natural man' is a deliberate act of creation, as indeed it must be if nothing is to be received through religious tradition. Who then creates? Answer – the creative personality. In the first instance the artist, the poet, and the visionary can set the pace. But in the long run, if all values are relative and all cultures different but equal, the creative personality comes to be the person with the most dominant will. Thus Rousseau puts us on a straight road to Nietzsche.

A Christian account of tradition and culture would of course be very different, and the recent writings of Alistair McIntyre on the development of tradition are highly relevant at this point. The question to be answered is whether it is possible to defend the idea of a great tradition, which includes and supports Graeco-Christian beliefs about rationality, and which proves its continuing worth by its ability to assimilate and use the best in other traditions. Whether or not such a defence of tradition is viable seems to me one of the key questions in the sphere of religion and politics today.

A third way of considering the religious/mythological co-ordinate in political life is in terms of its ability to provide social cohesion. This is a concept obviously relevant to the question of establishment, to which we shall come later, and there is a long sociological tradition which I do not need to expound, which interprets religion functionally in these terms. There is also a more immediately practical side to the question in Britain today, namely how far can the nation afford to move in the direction of multi-culturalism without taking care to safeguard at least some common values?

I would myself go further than this and assert the need also for a common language of hope, aspiration and penitence, not necessarily shared by all, but recognized by all as the formal language of the nation in moments when it is important to express some kind of national consciousness. A formal public commitment to religious faith at least provides a basis on which cohesion can be built.

There are no doubt other ways in which the religious/mythological co-ordinate can make its presence felt in the political sphere. My purpose has been simply to demonstrate a little of the variety, while indicating how its form and presence is affected by the strength of the other co-ordinates.

The rational critical co-ordinate received its most complete expression in the political thinkers of the Enlightenment. A key element in this was the rejection of religious authority and an attempted rejection of the whole mythological element in political thinking. Enlightenment politics was based on two assumptions. First that it is possible to decide on rational grounds what is 'best' for man, and secondly, rejecting the Platonic model, that it is not necessary to depend on a philosophical élite, but that all can be educated to follow enlightened self-interest. The almost universal acknowledgement of individual rights is one of the most enduring feats of this kind of thinking, but its limitations become all too apparent as rights proliferate and it becomes less and less plausible to claim that they are self-evident.

As already indicated, an inherent flaw in the Enlightenment programme as originally conceived was the assumption that what is 'best' for man can somehow be determined by an analysis of his 'true nature', which in turn can be disclosed by scientific discovery. This is a hope which has not been fulfilled and it is very doubtful whether it ever could be fulfilled. In fact the religious view that the fundamental nature of man systematically eludes complete description seems to be much nearer the truth.

We have already seen how one way of escaping from this dilemma was the substitution of culture for nature and how this in the long run opens the way for the powerful to attempt to remake man in whatever image they choose, in other words, tyranny.

The critical rational co-ordinate in politics is hugely important. Good government entails trying to act on rational principles and trying to defend policies on rational grounds. The moral basis of most public decisions is that most persuasive of the many attempts to create a rational ethics – utilitarianism, in one or other of its modern guises. But the lesson to be drawn from the Enlightenment, and what followed it, is that such a rational critical approach to politics cannot in the end answer the central questions about its own basic assumptions, and is thus vulnerable, either to takeover by some powerful ideology, or to a slide into moral and political indifferentism.

The pragmatic co-ordinate in political life is the one towards which conservative politics in Britain most naturally tends. Agonizing over the relationship between mythologies and rational principles can be dismissed as both a luxury and a danger. It is a luxury because 'reality' will dictate practical policies in the long run. It is a danger because religious enthusiasts and political theorists are inveterate tinkerers. They represent the desire to shape and to control, rather than to let be. They tend to assume greater knowledge than even the wisest of them actually possess, and their plans for ameliorating the lot of mankind are therefore inevitably defective.

Hayek provides a good illustration of conservative pragmatism. He sees the forces governing a large civilization – or what he terms 'an extended order' – as quite different from those operating in a relatively small face-to-face community. He presents a theory of how our present complex and 'successful' extended order has evolved 'by a process of unconscious self-organization'. He goes on to make the point that the variety, competitiveness and efficiency possible in such an extended order can only be harnessed effectively if it has also evolved certain moral traditions, backed by a mythology, which are sufficiently long-term to fit into an evolutionary timescale. In his own words:

> The extended order resulted not from human design or intention but spontaneously; it arose from unintentionally conforming to certain traditional and largely *moral* practices, many of which men tend to dislike, whose significance they usually fail to understand, whose validity they cannot prove, and which have nonetheless fairly rapidly spread by means of an evolutionary selection – the comparative increase of population and wealth – of those groups which happened to follow them. The unwilling, reluctant, even painful adoption of these practices kept these groups together, increased their access to information of all sorts, and enabled them to be fruitful and multiply.[1]

If Hayek is right, then the politics of practical necessity can no more escape paying attention to its religious/mythological co-ordinate than can the politics of critical rationalism. Hayek concentrates on the long-term evolutionary counterpoise to destructive self-interest but there are similar short-term considerations. Unrestrained pragmatic politics leads to the tyranny of the successful over the failures. It invites concentration on short-term goals at a time when the conditions of success require long-term planning, however inadequate the rational basis of such planning has to be as a consequence of human ignorance. Pragmatic politics also suffers from the danger of feedback. A successful extended order might operate unknowingly on Hayek's principles, but if it comes to understand itself consciously and exclusively in terms of those principles it runs the risk of destroying the mythology on which it depends. The mythology in other words has to be seen as having its own validity independent of its function in a Hayekean scheme of things.

This very brief and inadequate tour of a vast political panorama has, I hope, served to make the point that religion and politics are to be seen as inseparable as much from a political perspective as from a religious one. It will also be apparent I hope that there is no 'right' answer to the relation between them from the political side any more than there is from the religious side. In thinking about concrete issues therefore and notably about the relation between Church and state in England we need to begin where we are, and with the awareness that adjustments and confrontations may have wide repercussions within a complex balance of forces. Furthermore, since all three co-ordinates are necessary, wise policies will not seek to disturb the balance too drastically.

The establishment of the Church of England is one small part of that complex balance. It has demonstrated an ability to evolve over the years, but critics claim that its significance has now almost reached vanishing point and that what remains of it is by and large detrimental to the Church. Insofar as this claim is based on some theoretical understanding of what a proper relation between Church and state should be I would dispute it, for reasons which I have already explained at length. Insofar as the argument is about the actual significance and value of establishment, there are three considerations which weigh heavily with me and which encourage me to believe that there is room for still further evolution.

First, the existence of an Established Church is a permanent reminder of the religious basis of civil power. If a nationally based Church is careful not to forget its universal and Catholic roots then establishment can also be an effective symbol of the limits of nationalism. Clearly the existence of the establishment is not a major feature in practical politics as these are actually conducted today. It acts more as a last court of appeal.

Nevertheless, disestablishment would, I believe, have a major negative impact in that the nation would appear to be saying that it wished to repudiate its Christian heritage, whereas under present arrangements the establishment gives a moral and religious identity to the nation. Many may not share this, and it is generally not an explicit element in political decision-making, but all the same it would be strongly felt by its absence, and the continued presence of the Churches would not compensate for it.

Secondly, the establishment provides with the Crown a symbolic frame of reference whose importance is not limited to churchgoers. This is particularly apparent on great national occasions, but is not limited to them, nor does the Church of England nowadays carry this symbolic public role by itself. The ecumenical movement has broadened the base of the establishment to everybody's advantage, but it seems to me that there still needs to be a specific point of attachment to the state through a major partner in the ecumenical movement remaining established. It is all part of this picture that the relationship between the Crown and the Established Church should be close, and I think it likely that in the absence of an Established Church the Crown could become dangerously isolated, and exposed.

A third cluster of reasons in favour of retaining the establishment relates to the Church's ordinary pastoral role in providing public access to the Christian faith and in catering for very different degrees of religious commitment. Attempts to narrow the traditional openness of the Church of England are worrying features in today's scene. It is true that an open church with a large fringe membership can become complacent and it is also true that the actual survival of the Church depends more and more on a comparatively small number of activists. But to lose the breadth of vision and the wide tolerance which have generally been characteristic of the Established Church would, I believe, be a great impoverishment not only to the religious lives of many individuals but also to the political life of the nation. A good political life, as I have said more than once, needs good people of many different kinds to sustain it.

I therefore do not look for radical change in the present pattern of establishment unless this is forced on the Church of

England from the outside. The recurrent tensions between Church and state are for the most part healthy and can be seen as elements in a process of mutual learning and adjustment. I believe and hope that this is well understood on both sides.

Note

1. F. Hayek, *The Fatal Conceit* (Routledge 1988), p. 6.

Interlude
The Gulf War

Sermon preached at the Gulf War Service of Remembrance and Thanksgiving, St Mungo's Cathedral, Glasgow, 4 May 1991

Some words from the Book of Genesis have been haunting me in recent weeks. 'Shall not the Judge of all the earth do right?'

It is a question asked in hope, and in puzzlement. Hope – because the desire to do right, to see justice prevail, to root out wickedness, is not just a human dream, but takes us deep into the heart of God's purpose for his world. It is precisely because there *is* a Judge of all the earth that our striving for a just and peaceful world is not in the end, we believe, a vain delusion.

It was that hope – no doubt like all human aspirations mixed with other motives as well – which led into war to resist aggression. Today we give thanks for, and remember with pride, those in our armed services who paid the price which it exacted. Some paid it through death in combat. Some through the tragic errors and accidents which war inevitably entails, particularly a war of such rapid and complex movements. Their deaths, no less than the deaths of those who died fighting, are to be honoured and remembered for their role and purpose in this same striving to do right. We mourn with those who mourn. And we pray that through the darkness of their grief they may see the light of God's promise that nothing shall ultimately be lost, nothing wasted.

Others have paid the price for this hope of justice through injury, through the disruption of their lives, through the pain of separation and anxiety, and through the experience of fear and horror and devastation, whose scars may never be fully healed in this life. We give thanks that so many called to serve in the Gulf have returned to us. We give thanks for the training and bravery which enabled them to perform their tasks with such skill and professionalism. And we give thanks for the policy of restraint which, however tragically it some-times went wrong, embodied the wish to get the whole wretched business finished with a minimum of death and destruction.

But it is at this point that hope turns to puzzlement – and worse. 'Shall not the Judge of all the earth do right?' Behind the question lies not just hope, but a painful bewildered agonizing. What if doing the right thing not merely fails to stem the tide of suffering but actually extends or diverts it?

We find the question, as I have said, in Genesis in a strange and ancient story about Abraham, the father of faith for Jews and Christians and Muslims alike. Abraham is shown in the story as bargaining with God over the fate of two cities which God has said he will destroy for their wickedness. 'But surely', says Abraham, 'you are not going to destroy the innocent with the wicked! What if there are fifty righteous people in the city? Shall not the Judge of all the earth do right?'

'No', says God, 'I won't destroy it for fifty's sake.'

'What about forty-five?' says Abraham cajolingly.

'I won't destroy it for forty-five's sake.'

'Forty . . . thirty . . . twenty . . . ten.'

'No', says God, 'I will not destroy it for ten's sake.'

Abraham pushes his luck no further. The conversation ends. And the cities are destroyed. It is an extraordinary story.

Perplexities about innocent suffering go right back to the roots of our religious traditions, Jewish, Christian and Muslim. The theme of the story is the counterpoint – the horrific and seemingly inevitable counterpoint – to all our hopes of justice and our fumbling attempts to secure it. In the end guilty and innocent suffer together, and often the innocent more than the guilty.

That is why our solemn act of remembrance today has to go beyond thanksgiving to a sad acknowledgement before God of the appalling suffering which war and its aftermath have actually brought in their train: the losses of human life and the devastation in Iraq itself, still locked into an oppressive and evil dictatorship; the dreadful plight of the Kurds and Shi'ites, innocent victims not just of war itself, but of the false hopes of successful rebellion it raised in their minds; the black clouds over Kuwait, and the oil-sodden Gulf. Who can forget the dying cormorants? And we think of the fearful and intractable political problems which still remain, not least in securing the future for Palestinians and Israelis alike.

How do we measure all these against what has actually been achieved? Abraham's agonized question echoes through the centuries. Must the hope of justice always be blighted by its frightful cost?

Faith answers, No. Faith that there *is* a justice in the world's affairs, that there *is* a Judge of all the earth, should make us humble and self-critical, acutely conscious of our need of God's mercy and forgiveness. But it should also guard us against being cynical.

Faith should increase our determination to build on the new hopes of international co-operation which this war has generated. It is easy for critics to scoff at the role played by the United Nations. Isn't it better, isn't it truer to the demands of faith, to keep alive the hope that, despite all the ambiguities, our world can sometimes find ways of uniting around a cause which it believes to be right?

It is easy to feel frustrated and dejected about the political complications in trying to protect the rights of minorities. Isn't it better, isn't it truer to the demands of faith, to rejoice in the fact that something, however little, can actually be done, and is being done, to renew hope among those on the edge of despair?

There were times in the crisis when it looked as though political conflict might easily spill over into religious conflict. Thank God it didn't happen. Christians, Muslims and Jews, both in this country and in the Middle East, wisely refused to let it happen – despite the anguish of conscience many of them were experiencing. Our different faiths impel us all to look beyond immediate political pressures for signs of hope in God. And the signs are there. May God give us the courage to find through them a deeper respect for one another and a more sensitive understanding.

But still the frightful cost in human lives and well-being can seem to mock our fragile hopes. For Christians there is only one final answer to Abraham's dilemma. The mystery of innocent suffering lies at the very heart of Christian faith. Abraham could only plead and wonder. Jesus, himself the innocent sufferer in a city he knew was doomed, revealed all suffering as encompassed within the suffering of God.

Faith must not disguise or evade the awfulness of war and the atrocities to which it can give birth. But it can look beyond them, beyond the legitimate pride in a task accomplished, beyond the sad mistakes and the unintended consequences. It can look beyond them to the day when our fallible human judgements will give way before the judgement of God, when death will be swallowed up in Christ's victory over the grave, when there will be no more tears, no more sorrow, and when God will be all in all.

PART

4

The Church of England

_____ 13 _____

Catholicity

_____

The Michael Ramsey Memorial Lecture, delivered at the University of Durham, 28 November 1990

One of the minor and less publicized duties of the Archbishop of York is occasionally to show parties of visitors round Bishopthorpe Palace. On open days in particular they come in great numbers, and from far and wide. In the drawing-room I explain to them that this is where we hang the portraits of the twentieth-century archbishops, and I invite them to tell me how many of them they can recognize. The look of alarm on many faces gradually subsides into a smile. 'Why, of course – there's Michael Ramsey.' Frequently he is the only one to be identified with any certainty, apart from myself – and that's not too difficult. Always somebody knows him. Often many people know him. And I cannot recall a single group of visitors among whom he has failed to be recognized.

He was, and is, enormously memorable, not only among those who were privileged to know him personally, but among countless others who may never have seen him in the flesh yet who regarded him as the very essence of what an archbishop should be – holy, wise, forceful and gentle, learned and simple, a man of God.

I feel privileged, therefore, to be invited to perpetuate his memory in this place which he loved so much, by inaugurating the Michael Ramsey lectures. It is a happy coincidence that the Archbishop of Canterbury was able to announce a fortnight ago the success of his appeal to found a Michael Ramsey chair of theology in the University of Kent, and it is hoped that the first appointment will be made next year. North and south will thus, each in its own way, but with the north as usual in the lead, have a continuing reminder of a much loved scholar, bishop and friend. I thank those, particularly the Governing Body of St Mary's College, who have taken the initiative in founding these lectures, and I am sure they will prove to be a series worthy of the man.

The title I have chosen, Catholicity, is intended to encapsulate, as far as one word can, the essence of the man. It is also the title of a report prepared in 1947 by a group of Catholic-minded theologians at the request of Archbishop Geoffrey Fisher. Michael Ramsey, then Van Mildert Professor here in Durham, was elected chairman of the group, and seems to have been the main author of the report. It owed much to his classic, *The Gospel and the Catholic Church*, written ten years earlier. Both reflected a lifelong concern with unity, a bringing together of what he then saw as the fragmented and lop-sided versions of Christian truth into a genuine Catholicism.

I have a further reason for choosing Catholicity as my theme. There is no doubt that many Catholic Anglicans feel beleaguered in the present climate of opinion, and wonder what future their particular concerns might have in the Church of England. Many feel, not entirely without reason, that they have been cast in a mainly negative and obstructive role, and that the glories of Catholic tradition, glories which were so apparent in Michael Ramsey's own life and teaching, have somehow been obscured.

I tried to express this at the end of an essay written two years ago in comment on the tragic Gareth Bennett affair. I am going to quote the relevant paragraphs as a kind of text for the main themes which I want to explore in this lecture.

It needs to be recognized that there are weaknesses in contemporary Anglo-Catholicism which make it hard to see how those who at present feel themselves marginalized can quickly recover a more significant position.

This is sad and ironic, because in the long-term the future

lies with Catholicism. It must, because only Catholic tradition is rich enough and stable enough to be able to offer something distinctive to the world without being captured by the world. But it must be a Catholicism which is true to its highest vision, and hence broad enough, hospitable enough, rooted sufficiently in sacramental reality, confident enough in its inheritance to be able to do new things, diverse enough, and yet passionately enough concerned about unity, to be genuinely universal.

At the moment neither Roman Catholicism nor Anglo-Catholicism measure up to this standard. If Dr Bennett's Preface sidetracks his Catholic colleagues into further recrimination and introversion it will simply have done harm. A parish in my own diocese has, as I write this, advertised a Mass for 'the maintenance of Catholic Faith and Order in the Church of England' complete with a 'procession to the crowned statue of our Lady Queen of Heaven' and 'veneration of the relic of Saint Pius V'. I do not wish to carp at what is doubtless a sincere intention, but it is plain that the Catholic future cannot possibly lie in that direction.

Nor can it lie in the belief that there is some unchanging and unchallengeable core of tradition which, if only it can be preserved, will somehow guarantee true catholicity. Catholic fundamentalism is no more viable than biblical fundamentalism, and no more capable of being validated by historical enquiry. True catholicity belongs as much to the future as to the past. It entails the creative development of tradition as well as humble respect for it.[1]

Implicit in this is a distinction which I believe has to be drawn between Catholic Anglicanism and Anglo-Catholicism. It is a distinction which underlies Dr William Pickering's recent and devastating sociological study of Anglo-Catholicism. Of course the connections between the two are intimate and complex. The influence of the Oxford Movement, through the growth of Catholic practices and the absorption of a Catholic spirit, brought about the transformation of the Church of England. But that great achievement owes a huge amount to those Anglo-Catholics who were prepared to press on beyond the limits of the acceptable, and who found their ultimate authority and rested their ultimate hopes, not in

Canterbury but in Rome. Yet, as Pickering points out, their very successes sowed the seeds of their own destruction. To the degree to which it remained a movement which restored Catholic consciousness to the Church of England as a whole, the Catholic movement could remain true to its vision and gradually lose its distinctiveness. But as a party within the Church of England, locating much of its authority in another Church, it was and is in danger of succumbing to intolerable ambiguities.

This is how Pickering describes it:

> In Anglo-Catholic terminology, it is common to refer to one member of the Church of England as 'Catholic' and another as 'just Anglican'. Indeed, to this very day it is not unknown for someone to say: 'I'm not Anglican; I'm Anglo-Catholic,' or even: 'I'm not Anglican; I'm Catholic.' It is clear from such statements that not all members can be called Catholic in the sense in which Anglo-Catholics use the word. Those who are Catholic are so by self-designation. The dilemma is this. The Church of England must be Catholic, since it adheres to the Scriptures, the creeds, and the ecclesiastical orders of bishops, priests, and deacons created by apostolic succession. Hence the Church is Catholic and all members must therefore be Catholic. Yet not all are Catholic! But numerically most are just 'ordinary C. of E. people'. What kind of Catholicism is it when in the one church some are held to be Catholic and some are not? Quite recently there was a letter in the *Church Times* which began: 'Sir, As a Catholic in the Church of England I find . . .'. The Federation of Catholic Priests composed a constitution in 1917 which started: 'The Federation is for Catholic Priests in communion with the See of Canterbury'.
>
> To make matters more complicated there are held to be degrees of Catholicism amongst Anglo-Catholics. Thus, one person is 'fairly Catholic' and another is 'very Catholic'. Anglo-Catholics actually disagree amongst themselves as to who among them is 'truly' Catholic and who is not.[2]

'Catholic' here seems to be synonymous with a certain style, rather than with ecclesial reality. And there is a similar problem with the locus of authority. As one Anglo-Catholic commentator put it: 'All the compasses went crazy after

Vatican II.' If Rome threw off many of the things which stylistically had made Anglo-Catholicism distinctive, where was it now to find its identity and purpose?

The retreat into defensiveness and negativity seems to be one response to this dilemma. And even the once special relationship with Rome has been threatened by Rome's increasing openness towards other Churches.

Pickering sums it up in these words:

> In this way the Anglo-Catholic position has been bypassed and their servile following of what they held was essentially a Roman Catholic doctrine in the matter of church order has been made to look silly. Further, in negotiations between the churches, the Anglo-Catholics are not going to receive a privileged place within Anglicanism. In no way can it be said that Anglo-Catholics and Anglo-Catholics alone speak for the Church of England. The old dilemma of Anglo-Catholicism being a party within a church rears its head once again. Furthermore, it has been a party that has constantly looked backwards and not forwards and in so doing has had much of its ground cut from beneath its feet.[3]

How then can our future as the Church of England lie, as I believe it must, with Catholicism? Here I return to my distinction between Catholic Anglicanism and Anglo-Catholicism. The need as I see it is to reaffirm the Catholicism *of* the Church of England and to draw out the implications of that, rather than to strengthen a particular party *within* our Church. It may seem unecumenical to concentrate thus on the Church of England. However I do so not in any exclusivist sense, but because that is where the problem lies. And I return to Michael Ramsey because that is how I believe he would have understood it.

Catholicism affirms the givenness and universality of the gospel, and its embodiment in a living community. It is rooted in the fidelity of God who remains true to his purposes at all times and in all circumstances. And it is focused in the person of Jesus Christ from whom gospel, Church and the special Christian character of faith in God take their origin, and by whom they are judged.

That is a large statement. It entails a certain way of treating history, to which I shall return. But it also entails a certain way

of treating the world as the whole field of God's activity. It is
this largeness of spirit and breadth of concern which I was
pointing to in my earlier statement, and which has often
seemed so notably lacking in much of today's climate.

Here Michael Ramsey can help us. I quote almost at random
a sentence or two from a lecture on F. D. Maurice:

> Theology is about every man. In the old words of St
> Irenaeus: 'the vision of God is the glory of man' [Favourite
> words of Michael Ramsey's which were to be placed on his
> memorial]. The Church has always professed to know this
> but has not always shown that she knows it with Maurice's
> shocking simplicity. If today there is a more vivid awareness
> that theology, in being about God, is also about every man,
> woman and child, then Maurice is rejoicing.[4]

He can help us too in our use of the past as a resource for the
present and future. Owen Chadwick said of him, 'The best of
all his talks had a historical slant.'

I was one of the privileged few at the famous dinner party,
just before his retirement, when he recounted a dream of
imaginary conversations at a sherry party with all his
predecessors as Archbishop of Canterbury. It is one of the
great regrets of those of us who were there that nobody had a
tape-recorder. We enjoyed the humour of a mind steeped in
history, consciously delighting in the communion of saints, as
well as the not so saintly. They were, after all, archbishops. To
be fussed by Fisher, mildly rebuked by Cranmer for the ASB,
and to find community of mind and spirit with Anselm, was a
rare experience.

The Gospel and the Catholic Church begins with an uncompromising assertion about the historical roots of faith: 'The
underlying conviction of this book is that the meaning of the
Christian Church becomes most clear when it is studied in
terms of the death and resurrection of Jesus Christ.'[5] The fact
of the Church, as he expounds it, is included in the fact of
Christ. And the controlling text throughout the first part of
the book, a text which brings together both the historical and
the universal dimensions, is 'One died for all, therefore all
died'. In those seven words lie the basis of Christian existence,
and Christian unity.

We are one in Christ because Christ identified himself with

our humanity. We are a new reality in Christ, because Christ died and rose again for us and with us, gathering us up into his own self-offering and his risen life. All this is given to us in the fact of Christ.

It follows that at the heart of the gospel there is a givenness, an objectivity, expressed for us in historical terms through the existence of the Church and the givenness of the sacraments.

Protestant Christianity with its suspicion of sacred forms, and saints, and holy places, and sacred institutions, may seem to deny these expressions of givenness on the grounds that nothing must come between the individual believer and God. But this is to make central a truth, which, while it may serve as a valuable corrective against corrupt ecclesiasticism, can fall into its own errors of subjectivity and sentimentality.

Catholic and Protestant need each other. The evangelical protest has to be taken up within the fuller truth to which Catholicism witnesses. I quote from the famous chapter on Ecclesia Anglicana:

> The Anglican church is not committed to a vague position wherein the evangelical and the catholic views are alternatives, but to the scriptural faith wherein both alternatives are one . . . Her bishops are called to be, not judicious holders of a balance between two or three schools, but without any consciousness of party, to be servants of the Gospel of God and of the universal church.[6]

In *Catholicity*, written ten years later, the starting-point is expressed in rather different terms. There is an opening reference to what the report calls 'the primitive unity created by our Lord'. This unity, we are told, 'consisted not only in unity of organization or in the promise of a world-wide universality, nor yet in the bond of charity: it consisted rather in a whole way of life which included belief, worship and morals.' The report goes on to spell this out in some detail, and the implication is that there was some primitive package, a quite full and well-articulated package, which somehow constituted the wholeness of the original tradition. True Catholicity lies in this wholeness, and ecumenism is an attempt to rescue it from its present fragmentation. 'The faith once delivered to the saints' need not involve a cast-iron uniformity, but it does require adherence to certain divine facts of which the Church and its outward order are an essential part.

It seems to me that this is saying rather more than Michael Ramsey was saying in his original book. In *The Gospel and the Catholic Church* he was describing Catholic faith and order as implicit in the death and resurrection of Christ. In Jesus' identification with humanity, the new Israel came to be, and the subsequent ordering of the Church is the outworking of that original identification. In *Catholicity* the implication appears to be that the entire package was in some sense given by Jesus to his disciples, and that in consequence the shape of the Catholic faith was to that extent explicit from the beginning.

This is where the doubts begin, and where forty years of critical scholarship have profoundly changed the picture. Was there in fact ever a primitive unity? Were there not from the start different interpretations of Christ which diverged and coalesced and only gradually assumed the shape and order in which they are now familiar? When the author of Jude referred to 'the faith once delivered to the saints' – a text which reverberates through my postbag like a clarion call – the Church was already well-established and was beginning to defend itself against what were presumably Gnostic speculations. It now seems overwhelmingly likely that the idea of a package of faith and practice which had to be defended grew out of such controversies, rather than being actually delivered in some relatively complete form by Christ himself.

The difference is between two interpretations of the given content of the Christian faith. I draw this over-simple contrast between two books to make the point that perhaps the simpler starting-point in the earlier book has more to commend it. Christian faith and practice grow out of the fact of Christ. Catholicity is the way of responding to this by setting it in its richest and most comprehensive context. And that context requires the living community of believers, not least because this is the only way of escaping from our own subjectivity. But the actual forms in which Christianity has developed can and do vary, not just through sinfulness and division, but because the fact of Christ, and the possibilities of response to that fact, positively invite diversity. Just as a parable is not exhausted by a single interpretation, no more is the story of Jesus. The Catholic aim is to contain this diversity within a single worshipping community, so that it enriches rather than divides, stimulates rather than alienates.

Theologians from Durham will have no difficulty in recognizing that what I have just been saying owes much to Stephen Sykes. I am attracted by his idea of Christian doctrine as what he calls 'an essentially contested concept', an authoritative focus – in this case the life, death and resurrection of Jesus Christ – which constantly generates, not pointless wrangles, but genuinely creative disputes. Different interpretations are held in relation to one another, and enabled to be creative, by the scripturally-centred worshipping life of the Church. I quote from his final summary in *The Identity of Christianity*:

> The argument has been that internal doctrinal conflict may actually serve a constructive purpose in the Church so long as there is a tradition of communal worship, centrally authorized, in which the symbols and rituals of the Christian faith are openly spoken and performed, and the whole Christian community opened up to the interior dimension of the self-offering of Jesus. It is when this is being carried out that theologians may have the confidence to make the necessary experiments and to risk making the necessary mistakes. The potential tyranny of intellectuals, with their superior articulacy and natural concern for the epistemology of the arguments on which they are called to adjudicate, is qualified by the context in which they are now seen to be working.[8]

His argument is about theology and theologians, but I believe it also has something to say about Catholicity. It seems to me that it is precisely within this broad vigorous life of the believing community, sustained by the Scriptures and a tradition of worship, that the true heart of Catholicity is to be found. I suspect that none of us will know it in its fulness until our traditions of worship and our readiness to hear one another begin to unite us rather than to divide us.

There is, however, a broader question underlying what I have been saying. This concerns the significance of tradition itself, not just in the Church, nor in theology, but in the whole of life and in relation to all our knowledge. A modern defence of Catholic tradition has to start with a deeper appreciation of the role of tradition as such than was possible forty years ago. And this, I believe, provides a more hopeful starting-point than was possible then for what Catholically-minded Christians want to maintain.

I turn to the work of Alister McGrath, an Evangelical scholar whose 1990 Bampton Lectures, *The Genesis of Doctrine*, seem to me to provide just the kind of intellectual basis which could restore a critically-minded Catholic self-confidence. The book is an enormously learned exposition of the historical credentials of Christian doctrine and its dependence on community tradition. He builds on, and criticizes, the work of Lindbeck on the nature of doctrine,[9] who succeeded in demonstrating how it has to be seen as part of a total culture, the language of a particular community which understands itself in terms of certain stories, images, practices, and relationships. Lindbeck developed the idea of doctrine as a kind of grammar for discourse within the community of faith. This is illuminating, though it can hardly be claimed that it is the way the original framers of doctrine actually thought about it.

McGrath presses home questions about the truth and validity of such a belief structure. He takes seriously the claim that all thought is historically located and socially conditioned, and that there is no Archimedean point from which it is possible to stand outside all community traditions and evaluate their truth. All claims to truth suffer from the same defect. Nevertheless, there are ways of being responsive to our foundation stories, and of allowing these to interact with present Christian experience, and serve as a corrective to such experience, which can give us confidence that traditional Christian doctrine is genuinely faithful to its origins in Christ.

He has some interesting comments on the role of doctrine in defining the boundaries of communities. Until comparatively recent times the Church of England has not felt the need for much doctrinal definition because it has not been concerned to assert an identity as other than the Church of the nation; it has located itself within English society as a whole. The Church in medieval Christendom occupied a similar position and was equally supine in doctrinal matters. But all that is now changing. The pressures on Churches to be distinctive are increasing, and the resulting controversies about doctrine are a consequence, at least in part, of their changed social circumstances, and of the need for self-definition. The paradoxical sectarianism of some forms of Catholicism can perhaps best be understood in these terms.

Furthermore Churches now have to operate in a secular intellectual climate which does not welcome the idea of locating the source of authority in the past, yet is curiously blind to its own dependence on inherited traditions. The Enlightenment thinkers tried to make the past redundant, but can now be seen to be as firmly locked in their own past, and in the social circumstances of their times, as those whose authority they sought to undermine.

There is a nice parallel in the hopes of the early American colonists who wanted to leave the corruptions, and entanglements, and pressures of their European past behind them to found a new world which was free from sin. If things went wrong there was always a new frontier to cross, and it was still possible to leave each newly settled world behind. Until there were no more frontiers. Then, in the words of Thomas Merton who developed this analogy, 'America gradually became the prisoner of that curse, the historical memory, the total consciousness of an identity responsible for what had happened.'[10] He looked towards the end of the American myth: 'What will we do when we finally have to realize that we are locked out of the lone prairie and thrust forth into the world of history along with all the other people in the world?' The time came sooner than he expected. The past has a habit of catching up on us, because it is a vital ingredient of what we are.

Indeed even in the most enlightened circles much of people's understanding of themselves and their times is consciously or unconsciously shaped by their history. Simon Schama in his wonderful book *Citizens: A Chronicle of the French Revolution* demonstrates again and again how the revolutionaries who were self-consciously trying to create a new world, interpreted what they were doing quite openly and deliberately in terms of imagery derived from the history, or mythology, of ancient Rome.[11] The story of Rome was both an interpretation and a justification for what they were doing in cutting off peoples' heads.

Alasdair MacIntyre has taken the theme of our dependence

on tradition even further.[12] Even rationality itself, he says, and hence all our criteria of evaluation, cannot escape from historical contingency. No matter how much we deny the significance of tradition, each of us is formed by and dependent on an historical process from which we can only partially escape. And this historical conditioning reaches down into the very way we think. This need not entail that all traditions are of equal value. Some clearly have the possibility of comprehending others. There can be greater or lesser traditions, broader or narrower ones. There can be dialogue between traditions, though it is much more difficult than it seems. The main point to be grasped, for my present purpose, is that there is nothing intellectually disreputable in holding an understanding of truth as conveyed within a community which constantly renews itself by an interplay between its original sources, its history, and contemporary understandings of its own experience and the reality in which it is set. There remains the haunting problem of rival traditions and how to judge between them. But here, it seems to me, the striving for Catholicity in its broadest sense is a good pointer to the ability of a tradition to go on developing and enriching itself by hearing and receiving from others. And I would add my own word here about the necessity of including the tradition of scientific rationality.

I return to McGrath who, for all his Evangelical antecedents, ends up with a Catholic doctrine of the Church.

> The Christian faith [he tells us] does not come into existence in a conceptual vacuum, but is both generated and informed by a corporate tradition – the proclamation of the community of faith . . . while the Christian tradition has tended to stress that it is none other than God himself who is the ultimate cause of faith, its more immediate cause is the proclamation of the community of faith. Indeed underlying the affirmation, 'I believe in Christ', may be detected a latent, 'I believe in the Church'.[13]

He goes on, 'The Christian faith is made available to us through a historical tradition, transmitted and propagated through a community of faith, and shaped by the manner in which that community worships and prays.'

Michael Ramsey would, I believe, have welcomed those

words. And despite all the theological and cultural changes which have taken place in the fifty-four years since his first theological classic was published, he would have recognized them as saying for our own day essentially what he was saying then.

Notes

1. J. Habgood, *Confessions of a Conservative Liberal* (SPCK 1988), pp. 90–1.
2. W. S. F. Pickering, *Anglo-Catholicism: A Study in Religious Ambiguity* (SPCK 1989), p. 143.
3. ibid., p. 260.
4. A. M. Ramsey, *Canterbury Pilgrim* (SPCK 1974), p. 43.
5. A. M. Ramsey, *The Gospel and the Catholic Church* (1936; SPCK 1990³), Preface.
6. ibid. (1990 edn), p. 209.
7. Jude 3.
8. S. W. Sykes, *The Identity of Christianity* (SPCK 1984), p. 285.
9. G. A. Lindbeck, *The Nature of Doctrine: Religion and Theology in a Postliberal Age* (SPCK 1984).
10. T. Merton, *Conjectures of a Guilty Bystander* (Sheldon 1977 edn), pp. 32–8.
11. Simon Schama, *Citizens: A Chronicle of the French Revolution* (Viking 1989), e.g. p. 861.
12. Alasdair MacIntyre, *Whose Justice? Which Rationality?*. Duckworth 1988.
13. Alister McGrath, *The Genesis of Doctrine* (Blackwell 1990), p. 178.

14

Believing and Belonging

Diocesan Newspaper, April 1991

Twice in recent months hostile columnists in both the national and the local press have stated that for membership of the Church of England it does not really matter what a person believes. This is a mischievous untruth. Mud, however, has a habit of sticking. Since questions of belief are obviously important in the Decade of Evangelism I want in this letter to try to clear up some confusions on the subject.

Those who would like to go deeper into it will find a lot of help in the two most recent reports of the Doctrine Commission. The first, entitled *Believing in the Church* and published in 1981, is about what it calls 'the corporate nature of faith'. It spells out at some length the way in which the community of faith understands the meaning of its own message, life, and history through its worship, creeds, teaching and behaviour. The second report, entitled *We Believe in God* and published in 1987, is much more of an invitation to individuals to explore their own personal faith in the light of Christian tradition.

The difference is significant. Corporate faith, the faith of the Church, has to be embodied, not only in what the Church is and does, but also in public documents. The faith of all Churches is grounded in the Scriptures. Most Churches accept the creeds as providing the authoritative interpretation of the Scriptures on certain crucial matters, notably the doctrines of the Trinity and of the nature of Christ. Most Churches also have a further set of documents which describe in more detail the stance of that Church on particular issues which have been significant in its history, and may go further than this in providing a kind of primer for Christian believing and living.

In the Church of England the Thirty-nine Articles and the Book of Common Prayer have performed this latter function. The Articles relate specifically to the main controversies at the time of the Reformation in the sixteenth century. The Prayer Book expresses doctrine through worship, thus making the profound point that doctrine is much more than just a matter of 'ideas in the head'; it is the basis for adoration and commitment. Foundation documents like these change slowly, if at all, and part of the Church's task is to make sure that this rich reservoir of belief and experience is not squandered.

A Church like our own, which for centuries was accepted as the normal vehicle for articulating faith in a broadly Christian nation, can exist for a long time without having to think too much about its faith or spell it out more clearly. This is one of the main reasons why Anglicans have not been too concerned with doctrinal definition. The doctrine has been there, in the bloodstream as it were, and there has been no need for greater precision.

But as our society has changed, and as familiar Christian assumptions have been questioned, the need for definition has increased. And definition always entails controversy. A truth which can be contemplated silently in prayer and felt on the pulses in worship, may be interpreted in a variety of ways when the attempt is made to set it out in a logical statement. Such differences of understanding are not a symptom of doctrinal weakness, but are inevitable if there is to be a proper recognition that the truth of God is greater than all our formulations of it.

Corporately, then, the Church of England has a steady tradition which slowly develops, which is encapsulated in our liturgy, and which at present is under pressure to become firmer and clearer now that it can no longer be taken for granted. Some members will urge a need for even greater firmness and clarity. Others will warn against losing the fundamental insight that worship and life can convey what words and formulae cannot. But to suggest that in the face of these pressures the Church of England is losing its grip on its doctrinal tradition is preposterous. To many Christians outside it, it is not the radicalism of the Church of England which worries them but its immobility.

By contrast individual belief has always had greater flexibility. This is inherent in the understanding of faith as personal response to a personal reality. Something unique from ourselves enters into our relationship with God. Personal faith is not just an echo of corporate faith, but each individual's way of actively grasping it and living it. There is bound, therefore, to be variety, but if it degenerates into idiosyncrasy and chaos then something has gone seriously wrong. The Church is not a free-for-all, any more than an orchestra is a free-for-all. We play the same work but with different instruments, and our commitment to playing the same work is expressed in our willingness to worship together.

The main test of orthodoxy in the Church of England, therefore, has always been willingness to worship in the forms which the Church provides. This does not mean literal adherence to every word in every service. Liturgy is a kind of poetry which conveys its meaning partly through direct statements, but also partly through symbols, nuances and resonances. To join in public worship is to open oneself to many levels of meaning. See how in the Easter services, for example, the thought moves backwards and forwards between Christ's resurrection and our own. To join in public worship is to intend what the Church intends without needing to spell out in precise detail how this is understood. It is to allow God to set one's individual gifts and one's own partial perceptions in the larger context of the life of his Body.

To describe this subtle interplay between individual and corporate faith, between living experience and inherited tradition, as 'believing what one likes', is simply dishonest.

15

Marketing the Church of England

Lecture delivered at the Annual Conference of the Chartered Institute of Marketing, 29 November 1990

I have an unfortunate habit of accepting invitations to talk about subjects on which I know very little. I do this on the principle that it is good to try to learn new things, and that to have to face an expert audience at least concentrates the mind. But I ought to have realized before I started that there is a difference between marketing and selling. I was originally under the impression that my topic was selling, and I felt that I was on safe ground because clergy are constantly being reminded that they are in sales not management. However I now realize that marketing is different. I shall therefore start with a brief look at three of the key concepts which I see as underlying it, and try to pinpoint the dilemmas which they pose for me.

I begin with the definition of marketing from some of your own literature:

1. 'Marketing is concerned with ensuring that the company provides what the customers want to buy.'

In a commercial organization that is obviously good sense. There is no point in trying to sell what people do not want to buy. It has some validity too in relationship to religion. To apply the marketing principle to religion entails identifying religious needs, and it is not hard to put together a list of human needs which are in some sense satisfied by religion:

Everyone needs a sense of purpose in life. They need to feel that their life has meaning, and quite a large part of religion is about this search for meaning.

Everybody needs an identity, some way of answering those awkward questions, Who am I? What is my life about? What am I doing here?

Everybody needs some way of coping with those feelings of dependence which we all experience when we are most conscious of our own weakness and frailty, and of our need for some resource outside ourselves.

Everybody needs support to assure them that they are not alone. They need some affirmation of what they are. They need something to boost their feelings of self-worth so that they can be assured that they matter, despite appearances and despite the many things that go wrong.

Everybody needs a community to which to relate, a sense of belonging somewhere within a fellowship of people who care about them.

Everybody needs a challenge. Everybody needs some expressions of idealism to respond to, and everybody at times needs acceptance and forgiveness and an assurance that the past need not close in on them and wreck the future, but that it can be taken hold of and transformed.

There are thus plenty of needs to which religion responds. However the danger of this need-centred approach to religion is that it may lock people in that very self-centredness from which it is supposed to deliver them. We are thus faced with a paradox. The needs which religion satisfies have to be met by looking away from them in some other direction. So there is an initial difficulty with the notion of marketing simply as a response to needs.

There is also a second difficulty in the definition of marketing with which I started. The concern is to ensure that the company provides what the customer wants to buy. But how far when dealing with religion is it possible or desirable to tailor the product to meet the customer's needs? Of course people do. People make up their own religions to satisfy their needs, but the official name for that way of going about things is idolatry.

One of the awkwardnesses of religion is that there is a sense in which it is simply 'given'. It makes its presence felt as a set of uncomfortable truths, or an uncomfortable reality, which demands a response. This is true in particular of the Christian religion, at the very heart of which is the notion that God takes an initiative towards us rather than that we take an initiative towards him. We are asked to respond to what he has already done. Admittedly the possibilities of that response have to be presented in ways which match human need and our present day understanding of the kind of world in which we live. But there is only a very limited sense in which it is possible to make a religious faith adaptable to consumer demand without changing its character to the point of destruction. So the initial problem is compounded.

2. The second element in marketing is, of course, competitive-ness. Now, I have no quarrel with competition as such. I know that it is the driving force of the market and that we are all involved in it. Furthermore, there is a conventional wisdom that competitiveness is good for religion too. It is claimed by some that the fact that there are different denominations puts each on its mettle to try to produce something a bit better and more attractive than the others. It is this kind of thinking which has led many sociologists of religion to interpret Christian ecumenism not as a sign of strength, but as a sign of weakness. As the Churches get weaker, so the story goes, they no longer have the inner self-confidence to compete with one another in an open market, and huddle together ecumen-ically against the chill winds of secularism. There is some truth in this, and I suppose one example of competitiveness producing vigour is the United States, where religion is a very popular and very competitive business.

However, it does not always work like this as a recent piece of research has made plain.[1] The research charts the growth and decline of all the churches in fourteen villages in the north of Northumberland over a period from the mid-seventeenth century up till 1981. The total population of the fourteen villages in 1850 reached its peak of 17,500 and since that date has declined to its present level of 7,000. The period from 1850 to 1900 was a time of very vigorous church building, particularly non-conformist chapels, and in competition with these many Church of England parishes enlarged their own church buildings. Thus by 1900 the total number of seats available in churches in those fourteen villages was no less than 13,000 by which time the population had already declined to about 10,000. In fact this increase had taken place from an original 8,500 seats at the very time when the population was declining, with the result that in 1900 there were 3,000 more seats than there were people. This was entirely the result of competition, and it is very evident from the parochial returns sent in to the then bishop that the clergy recognized this competition and complained about it again and again as undermining their position. It has been calculated that the maximum proportion of the population which could be in church at any one time is about 58%, since there are always people who have to work, as well as the sick, the house-bound, those with very young children, and of course, in the period in question, servants. Thus a population of 10,000 would effectively have 5,800 people to fill 13,000 seats. This means that the maximum possible 'pew occupancy' would be 45%, and the likely 'pew occupancy' less than 25%. Most churches must always therefore have looked empty, and empty churches breed a sense of failure. Those who sense that they belong to a failing institution are apt to lose their enthusiasm for belonging to it. Hence the pattern of decline.

Churches less than a quarter full also tend to be financially stressed. Unable to pay their clergy properly, they amalgamate and either arrange for one clergyman to serve several churches, or they close their buildings. Either policy leads to further losses and so a spiral of decline sets in simply through the operation of demographic factors and unwise competition. Still today in that part of Northumberland and after many church closures there are 6,500 seats for 7,000 people.

I give you this as an example of church decline actually brought about by competition. Nor is it an isolated example. Similar research in Lambeth a few years ago revealed a somewhat similar pattern. It would be foolish to claim that this is the only cause of church decline, but it is one of them which has only recently been recognized. The point is that competition is not necessarily helpful. There is a strength which comes from co-operation. Thus whatever kind of marketing we look for in the Church it should not, I believe, be brand marketing.

There may, however, be a place for competition with some of the other philosophies on offer in our present society. The chief among these being a kind of selfish individualism and consumerism. Indeed these have been a main source of complaint among the Churches over the past decade or so. But then the question has to be asked, Can this competition from consumerism be combated by making religion itself into a consumer product? There lies my second difficulty in the concept of marketing the Church of England.

3. My third difficulty concerns the inevitable relationship between marketing and profit. I am no more questioning profit as such than I am questioning competitiveness as such. Unless a company can make a profit it ought not to be in business at all. The profit motive makes things happen which could never happen without it, nor would I want to underplay the Church's dependence on a need for money, particularly among this audience. But within a religious context the financial support needs to be a by-product of commitment, rather than the main aim of commitment. If people once suspect that they are being converted in order to provide more cash to pay the vicar, that is the end of it.

Within the Church of England the financial situation is further complicated by the belief that it is an enormously wealthy Church and financially self-sufficient. The truth is curiously different. In fact, in comparison with some continental Churches it is comparatively hard up. The German churches, for example, are financed by a church tax paid by the majority of the population. Most Germans contract to pay 10% of their income tax to the church. This goes to all the churches in Germany which are in consequence extremely well provided for and capable of doing many things on a worldwide basis, which are well beyond the means of the Churches in Britain. Belgium, to take another example, is one of those countries which came under Napoleonic rule, and in which all the churches are now financed entirely by the state. When Napoleon took away all church endowments, he wrote it into the constitutions of the various states that their governments would be responsible for the building and maintenance of churches and for the salaries of the clergy. Thus the Roman Catholic cardinal is actually paid for by the Belgian government, a fact not generally known.

Our situation in the Church of England is that we provide a service for the whole nation. We have as many branches as there are post offices – more possibly. We are partly financed by endowments from the past, and that is where the so-called wealth of the Church of England lies, but nowadays these endowments only pay about half of what is actually needed to run a nationwide organization with a branch in every locality and village. All the rest comes from a quite small number of active church members.

This means that there is a strong case for adopting a church-need approach to finance. The Church needs money to keep on providing a service for the nation. However, the difficulty in this church-need approach is that it can distort the Church's basic message just as disastrously as the approach based on the appeal to individual needs. It is frequently said, 'They are only interested in your soul because they are after your money', and on seeing those endless thermometers outside dilapidated Victorian buildings, 'Why prop up a crumbling structure?'

So there is a strong negative message which comes through from appeals for money. Yet there may be a positive side to it too. I frequently notice this in villages where they have to raise, say, £50,000 to keep the spire on the church. The normal response is for the whole village to co-operate and thereby discover a new sense of purpose and identity through having raised money for the church, something which might never have happened if the spire had not been about to collapse. Money is always an ambivalent factor.

I have dwelt on these three difficulties in the marketing approach to make the point that tailoring products in a competitive spirit in order to make a profit is not an encouraging model for trying to sell the Church of England. Yet the television evangelists in the United States do all three of these things. They put over a message which will make their audiences feel good, warm, wanted and accepted. They are highly competitive, highly self-assertive and glitzy, and they persuade their audiences to pay for them on a massive scale. Is this an example of successful religion? Or the corruption of it?

After that depressing start let me be a bit more positive. What can the Churches learn from the skills of marketing? It is a question which is especially urgent as the possibilities of religious advertising on television begin to confront us. First, therefore, let me say a word about the product, then about the market, and then much more briefly about the method.

First the product. What is Christianity actually about? Or more generally what is religion about? In our kitchen there is a poster picture of the Grand Canyon and underneath is written, 'To wonder is to begin to understand'. Religion begins in wonder. It is also about beauty, and mystery, and holiness, and love; it is about the things which cannot be said because they lie too deep for words. There is a helpful way of thinking about religious faith as a kind of light, a light which may come from a single simple source, like the sun. Yet generally we see this light in terms of all the objects from which it is reflected, in fact in terms of the total complexity of the world which is illuminated by it. In much the same way the Christian faith is about the simplest thing in the world; it is about loving God and being loved by him. And it is also the most complex thing in the world because the reality of that love reflects on everything that is and everything that happens. Faith is as complex as the world in which we live, but it is also about a simple response to self-giving love as seen in the life, death and resurrection of Jesus Christ.

Another way of putting it is to describe religion as a way of life which entails believing – having a certain concept of what the world is about and what matters in it. It also entails belonging – it is a social and not just an individual matter. And it also entails behaving – it is about the kind of people we are and what we do. All this finds its focus in worship and it is only in the context of worship, which ultimately ends in silence, that the whole system of symbols and stories and promises and demands which make up the content of the Christian faith begin to make sense. It is in worship that we discover how belief is not just about the furniture in our minds, not just about opinions, but about the commitment of our very being, what we are, what we think and what we hope to be. It is in the context of worship that we discover that words are not just sounds which float in the air but can in some mysterious way point us to the *Word*, a life-changing Word, a Word which penetrates right inside us and makes us new people. In the context of worship we can see how actions, simple actions like taking bread and wine, can become sacraments which convey to us the very presence of God. It is in the context of worship that we can see how singing, often quite indifferent words to quite indifferent tunes, can become praise in which it is possible to lose oneself in response to God. It is in the context of worship that we can see how hopes become prayers and what in other contexts might be wishful thinking becomes life-empowering and sends us out stronger and more hopeful. It is in the context of worship that we can discover how membership becomes communion, an awareness of unity with each other, and with God, and with all humanity.

That in a word or two is the product we have to sell. It is a pretty complex reality. One can only invite people to enter it in ways which do not falsify it too much. To falsify it in order to encourage people to accept it is in the end to wound and distort their expectations. There is nothing worse than falsifying a product in a way which makes people say, 'I am never going to buy from that firm again'.

There are various types of falsity. It is easy to cheapen religion. I was sent an example the other day – a shock horror headline, 'Gay Vicar sex orgy with killer'. Underneath was written, 'Well it made you read it!' If you start like that it is very difficult to go on. Furthermore, it is easy to exploit misconceptions and stereotypes, among whom clergy, bishops and archbishops are the most popular sitting targets. There is another kind of falsity summed up in the word 'glamour'. The dictionary definition of glamour is 'a deceptive and fascinating quality about a person or place that attracts in spite of reality'. There is nothing gained by inviting people into religious reality unless you tell the truth, and the truth may be uncomfortable. There is a third type of falsity, namely fake simplicity and fake certainty. These are popular because most people want what they call 'a simple gospel', and we all long for certainty. But the sad truth about this world is that certainty is not to be had. There can be confident faith but there is no certainty anywhere. An over-simple banging of the drum can be very attractive in an uncertain age, but only a faith that enters into the ambivalancies and uncertainties of everyday life can be real in the long run.

There can nevertheless be simple pictures and simple presentations which do not falsify. Iconography in the Orthodox Church is a good example. Icons have a way of conveying in simple pictorial form some very deep spiritual truths. To the uninitiated they may seem no more than old pictures in churches, but to those who have learnt to read them they can communicate their meaning at a profound level. Thus people often look at icons and accuse the artists of not being able to draw in perspective. The fact is that many icons are drawn in what is called 'reverse perspective' so that the lines converge on the viewer rather than on the horizon. Why? Because the further we go into ourselves the smaller we are and the smaller our world is. The further we move out into the depth of the picture the bigger everything becomes until eventually it encompasses infinity. There is a spiritual lesson in that. Or again you may have noticed that icons frequently contain drawings of buildings which are architecturally impossible or broken. Why? Because these represent the crazy sort of world which people build for themselves, in contrast with the inner peace and calm of the figures of the picture who represent what is given by God.

How does all this relate to the Church of England? It seems to me that one of the major selling points of the Church of England is precisely the openness which this Church has always displayed towards actual complexity. That is one reason why it is such a puzzling body to so many people. This openness is conveyed among other ways in its character as a community church rather than an associational one. I have in mind the sociological distinction between a church which is related to the whole community in which it is set, and is open to serve it whether people are members or not. An associational church is formed, not just by being there, but by deliberate association, and usually has a defined and sometimes a closed membership.

The spirituality of the Church of England is rooted in a very English kind of consciousness. In its most typical spiritual writers there are certain easily identifiable characteristics. For the most part they are moderate, practical, homely, suspicious of priestliness, optimistic and with not too much dwelling on the fact of sin. These may not be the greatest spiritual characteristics in the world but they are serviceable ones. There is an order and dignity and beauty in worship. Still in most places these days there is a rootedness in English history and Catholic tradition which makes the Church both homely and universal. The negative side of all this is the danger of self-satisfaction, laziness, parochialism and nostalgia. Too many images of sunlit country churches and grand state occasions can reinforce self-delusion. Nevertheless it seems to me that the distinctiveness of the Church of England lies in its subtle relationship with the whole community as a place of resort for the sanctification of everyday life.

There, then, is the product we are trying to sell. What about the customers? I find it helpful to divide them into three categories.

First, there is the fringe. The people who are generally sympathetic towards the Church and who would, on the whole, put themselves down as members of the Church of England but are chiefly characterized by hardly ever attending it. Such people move in and out of a relationship with the Church under various personal and social pressures. Thus there are stages in the life-cycle, a tendency to move away, for example, in adolescence and back to the Church in old age. The effect of social trends on the fringe members can be shown by comparing church attendance in different denominations over a period of years. Attendances seem to move in cycles which are common to all the denominations, and this seems to indicate that some of the factors which most influence church attendance lie not in the churches themselves, but in society at large. Clearly in a local situation the personalities concerned can make a difference, but statistically it is major social changes such as increased mobility, weekending, periods of stress in national life, the current image of churchgoers, and, no doubt, many other factors which affect the way in which the fringe behaves.

The fringe is also very vulnerable to the downward spiral of decline which I have described in the Northumberland villages. Feelings of failure within a church induce more failure. Nevertheless the spiral of decline can be put into reverse, and recent experience of what is called 'church planting' is one of the more interesting examples of the way in which this can happen. Suppose there is a flourishing congregation in one parish and a dying church a few miles away. Part of the flourishing congregation can transplant into the dying church and as soon as the people there become aware of the signs of life, that church itself begins to grow. People who may have left in despair many years before come back in.

One can also see the influence of social pressures on the fringe by comparing churchgoing in different parts of the British Isles. Thus in percentage terms, for every one person in England who goes to church regularly there are two in Wales, three in Scotland and seven in Ireland. One obvious reason for this difference is that in Ireland religious allegiance is a major mark of social and national identity. In Scotland this is true to a lesser extent and in Wales still less. One of the peculiar characteristics of the English is the complacency about being English. Because we form the majority among the four nations there is not so much social need to express our identity in terms of religious practice, though the majority of English people would still think of themselves as 'C. of E.'

A second group of customers are the unchurched. These form the most difficult market because they belong to a social pattern which quite explicitly excludes religion, and has done so over many generations. This is particularly true of people who moved from the country into the cities during the Industrial Revolution, and were unchurched in the process. There are deep social patterns which exclude religion and ingrained feelings which have to be overcome before a religious message can be heard. Religious people are often thought of as 'them', and written off as a lot of middle class hypocrites.

There is nevertheless a popular religion even among the unchurched. This rotates around such phrases as, 'You don't need to go to church to be good.' Often there is enormous deprivation in terms of the language and symbolism which are needed in order to make sense of religion, yet even among the unchurched there remains an extraordinarily high level of belief in God (whatever that means) and morality (whatever that means) and Christian values (whatever they mean). It frequently happens that people who externally seem totally unchurched become annoyed if it is suggested that they are not Christian.

It seems to me that in trying to get a message through to such people one has to start by affirming what is there already, and drawing it out in a way that helps people to make sense of their own lives. I am increasingly impressed by the importance of the television soaps in providing for large numbers of people a mythology and series of stories in terms of which they come to a deeper understanding of themselves. In a curious way the television soaps have for many people taken on a quasi-religious role in providing this sense of identity, and I long for the day when we shall see a really serious treatment of religious themes in that kind of television production. More positive images of the Church in that context could, I believe, do a great deal to help the unchurched lose some of their misapprehensions.

Thirdly there is the up-market, and on this level I suspect marketing techniques are least likely to be effective. I see one of the great evangelistic tasks of our day in the more serious engagement by Christians in the intellectual, cultural and political life of the nation.

Finally, a word about methods. It seems to me that the most effective field for a marketing approach lies with the fringe, and here I would point to the latent idealism in many such people, particularly young ones. There is the attraction of 'causes'. There are the huge numbers of young people who will go to such places as the Taizé community, and find inspiration through a community which bears the marks of holiness, joyfulness, prayerfulness and simplicity. There is the attraction of outstanding Christian lives. There are specific challenges, such as the challenge to many young people to give a year of their lives to God in some form of unselfish service. There is the overriding challenge 'to take up your cross and follow me'.

Then there are the rites of passage. There are times in the life of everyone when they are open to the religious dimension of life in a special way, because they are going through a period of change or crisis or new responsibility. Many young couples rejoicing at the birth of their first baby are suddenly brought up sharp by the uncomfortable question, 'What kind of person are you going to bring it up to be?'

I have talked already about the need to change images. It would be helpful if the media sometimes showed pictures of full churches, not just for *Songs of Praise* and not just with arm-waving charismatics, but ordinary mixed congregations. It would be good to have dramas depicting sensible clergy grappling with real issues. It would be wonderful to enjoy religious reporting which was not obsessed with the sensational, the bizarre and the divisive.

Lastly, I leave you with the thought, 'Tell the truth but tell it slant'. Tell it through images, not by beating people over the head with it. Somehow we need to find ways of rehabilitating those powerful images which, through the centuries, have carried religious claims and made them meaningful to all sorts of people who are outside the inner worshipping life of the Church. Sometimes poetry can do this, and often it is done best through poets who are not explicitly Christian, but who can feel the seriousness of religious themes. In that way the theme can get through without any feeling that the reader or listener is being got at. I think particularly of a fine poem by Philip Larkin on church-going in which he described wandering round empty churches and feeling strangely attracted by them. Despite his own atheism he knew that he was in 'a serious house on serious earth'.[2]

As people begin to become aware of that kind of thing then we are in business.

Notes

1. R. Gill, *Competing Convictions*. SCM Press 1989.
2. P. Larkin, 'Church Going', in *Collected Poems*. The Marvell Press and Faber and Faber 1988.

Ruth

*Sermon preached to members of the General Synod in York Minster,
12 July 1992*

Ruth 1.16–17: 'And Ruth said, "Intreat me not to leave thee, or
to return from following after thee: for whither thou goest I
will go; and where thou lodgest I will lodge: thy people shall be
my people, and thy God my God: where thou diest I will die,
and there will I be buried: the Lord do so to me, and more also,
if ought but death part thee and me."'

It has to be read in the Authorized Version. Even so, there is a
certain irony in the fact that the most beautiful expression of
loyalty in the Bible – and perhaps in all literature – should have
been addressed to a mother-in-law.

Ruth's declaration of love for Naomi lifts a domestic tragedy
onto the high plain of spiritual drama. The point is that Ruth
was a foreigner. Naomi and her husband had been driven by
famine to move from Bethlehem to the hated land of Moab.
Their two sons had married Moabite women – Ruth and
Orpah. Tragedy had struck when husband and both sons had
died, leaving Naomi with two foreign daughters-in-law, and
no heirs. There was nothing more she could do for them, she
said. So she urged them to return to Moab while she went back
to Bethlehem. Orpah went. But Ruth clung to her in words
which have rung down the ages.

As the story unfolds we see this foreign girl who had lost
everything, her husband, her homeland, her future, gently
and tactfully winning the love of one of Naomi's kinsmen.
After three chapters of pastoral idyll, they marry. And the
final twist comes when in the last words of the book Ruth is
revealed as the great-grandmother of King David.

Orpah, meanwhile, had done the sensible thing, cut her
losses, and gone home. Jewish legend identifies her, with
extreme improbability, as the ancestress of Goliath. What

legend seems to be telling us is that reasonable decisions can sometimes be remembered as betrayals.

But what is the main story telling us? and why is it in the Bible at all? Here we find ourselves offered two diametrically opposed interpretations.

One way of reading it is as a story designed to expose the folly of religious exclusiveness. Its point is to be found in its shattering last verse – the genealogy which leads from Ruth to David. Its target is the narrow-minded Jewish reformers in the period after the end of the monarchy and the exile, at a time when faith was expressed in strict adherence to law. And none was more strict than the law against mixed marriages enforced by Ezra the scribe.

You hypocrites, the story is saying, you are forcing these people to get rid of their foreign wives. But David himself, David the hero king, David the archetype of the Messiah, was himself the great-grandson of a woman from Moab.

Like the book of Jonah, which carries the same message against religious bigotry, the story is satire. In Jonah it is humorous satire, strip cartoon exaggeration. In Ruth it is gentle satire, which relies on the reader's growing admiration for a character whom strict orthodoxy would reject.

That is one interpretation. The other is to read the story as an example of Jewish liberality. There is no question of rejecting this widowed foreigner. The fact that she was David's ancestress is incidental. The point lies in her loyalty to Naomi, in her clinging to the Jewish part of her heritage, in her seeing her future as part of the people of God. On this interpretation it is not the narrow-mindedness of some strands of Judaism which is under attack, but its universal appeal which is being celebrated.

Which interpretation is right? Perhaps they both are. Perhaps both are needed, because they belong to different contexts. And perhaps it is not just the Book of Ruth which can yield apparently contradictory insights. Scripture has this disturbing capacity to say different things to different people. Poetry does the same. Its meanings do not lie on the surface, but reverberate in the depths with what we ourselves bring to it.

To be aware of multiple meanings is not to surrender to anarchy. It is not a case of 'anything goes'. There are meanings which can honestly be found in the Bible, and meanings which cannot. But the awareness of multiple meanings can cure us from naively supposing that when we put questions to Scripture there is always something which can be described as *the* scriptural answer. It is this deeply false assumption which again and again has driven Christians into opposing camps, each claiming to possess the only truth.

If there were indeed unequivocal answers to the questions which bother us, there would be little need of synods – at which some might rejoice. The right answer would simply be there, like a plum for the picking. There could be no arguments.

But life and faith are not like that. Indeed one reason why they are not is that faith is for the most part given to us in stories and sayings which can bear different interpretations. So there can and must be study, discernment, and argument. We all bring something of ourselves, and of the traditions in which we stand, to this process. And we need each other if we are to see with more than one eye, and hear with more than one ear.

For those of us who belong to the General Synod, questions about how to make decisions on difficult issues have a special urgency. If even an apparently simple story like Ruth can be read in different ways by different people in different contexts, we need to be careful. Putting up roadblocks, occupying immovable positions, making incontestable claims, may be good for morale but bad for theological integrity. And this is true whatever label we give ourselves.

A better way, surely, is to fill ourselves with the stories of our faith and their multiple meanings, to think as hard as we can, to pray as hard as we can, to listen to one another as hard as we can, and then to decide in humble acknowledgement that we may be wrong. The only assurance we can have is that even if our best intentions lead us into error, we do not fall out of the hands of God.

We may find ourselves, like Orpah, making a sensible decision for the best possible reasons, only to be branded later as a betrayer. We may, like Ruth, cling unreasonably to a vision which has captured our loyalty, and find unexpectedly that the future lies in our hands. There is no escape from the risks of faith. Nor should there be, for God takes the risks of faith alongside us. He has pledged his loyalty to fallible creatures who frequently get things wrong. And he takes the wrongness onto himself. He has enclosed the risks within the promise of his own faithfulness. And he leads us, like Ruth, back to Bethlehem, where everything begins.

The Decade of Evangelism

Sermon preached at the commissioning of Michael Marshall and Michael Green for the Decade of Evangelism in St Paul's Cathedral, 23 September 1992

It is a happy, but unplanned, coincidence that this service takes place fifty years to the day from another great service in St Paul's, when the British Council of Churches was inaugurated under the presidency of William Temple. It was in the very darkest days of the war, just before Alamein, and it was a bold affirmation of hope in the Christian future. The Churches reached out towards a unity, all the more desperately needed if a shattered world was to be rebuilt. And in the days ahead they played an honourable part in that restoration of faith and hope and love.

We too live in difficult times, less dire than fifty years ago, but no less real. Our world is beset by new insecurities and injustices, our society often bewildered, divided and direction-less, and our Church suffering deep internal strains. So what better time could there be to renew our faith in the gospel, to hear again Paul's comforting words about being 'hard pressed on every side, but not crushed; perplexed but not in despair ', and to recapture the sense of urgency in having a message to proclaim which the world so desperately needs. And though this is primarily a Church of England occasion, we have not, please God, lost our ecumenical vision. It is good to have leaders of other Churches with us here this evening. The Decade of Evangelism is not a private Anglican possession, though some critics delight to present it as a shot in the arm for an ailing Church. In fact we are part of a movement of renewal and reaffirmation worldwide. The original inspiration for the Decade was the desire to celebrate two thousand years of our Lord. And the new life already bubbling up all over the place is a sign that the vision was timely and right.

It is in this context, then, of need, of hope, of togetherness, and in celebration of what has already begun, that we welcome and commission our two advisers, Michael Marshall and Michael Green. They have returned home, as it were, to offer the very special gifts God has given them, to help us in our task. And we give thanks to God for their willingness to enter into an exhausting, but we hope also exhilarating, peripatetic ministry, with a programme which already looks frighteningly full. They are going to need all the energy and resilience usually associated with springboards. And especially, they are going to need our prayers.

We give thanks, too, for those others, both within the Springboard initiative and throughout the dioceses, who will be supporting them in their work, and for those who have made all this financially possible through the Lambeth Partnership.

But what of their task? and of our task in working with them? No one would presume to tell them how to be evangelists. Earlier this summer Michael Green presented me with a 590-page book he has written on the subject – one of many. Both Michaels, in fact, are prolific authors, speakers and preachers, with ways of conveying the gospel message which strike home to the hearts of many.

I turn for guidance, therefore, to the archetypal evangelists, four of them, who were the first to tell the story on which our faith is based. My text, for what remains of this sermon, is no less than the Gospels of Matthew, Mark, Luke and John. I shall not read them out.

It has always been a puzzle that there were four. But the reasons for this have gradually become clearer as the study of the New Testament has deepened. They were writing for different constituencies at different times. They brought different theological interests and emphases to what they were doing. And they responded in different ways to the discussions and controversies going on in their churches at the time when they were writing. Already this tells us something about the diversity of the evangelistic task and the importance of relating it to the context in which it is undertaken.

Matthew's Gospel, for instance, is basically church-centred. It spells out in a way no other Gospel does the kind of demands which Christian discipleship places on the life of the Church and its members. It shows us Jesus the teacher. It is an appeal for stronger faith and obedience.

I am merely brushing the surface of an immensely complex subject, but the point is that part of the evangelistic task is addressed *to* the Church. We don't sit here having all the answers. We need Christ constantly to challenge and to change us, just as much as the world needs to be challenged and changed by him. And Matthew, not least in giving us the Sermon on the Mount, does just that.

Mark is in one sense even more challenging. Have you noticed how in St Mark's Gospel the disciples get an almost uniformly bad press? They bumble and fumble and misunderstand, not because they are especially foolish or wicked, but because they are face to face with a mystery too great for them. Mark is trying to explain, in the way he tells the story, why an event so tremendous as the coming of Christ could be ignored, misrepresented or rejected. Nevertheless, there are some who *do* understand – a madman, a foreign woman, a Roman soldier, outsiders all of them. True insight and genuine response come to and from the least likely people.

This is not a comfortable message for the Church. It makes the evangelistic task a subtle balance between giving and receiving, telling the story, opening up the mystery, and allowing it to reverberate in unexpected places.

Luke, by contrast, has it all worked out. He tells us so in his opening sentences. His account of the story of Jesus is engagingly down-to-earth. He sets it in the context of the worldwide mission of the Church, beginning with the Old Testament priesthood in Jerusalem, and ending in the heart of the Roman Empire. It is a story of triumph through suffering. We are shown the disciples being consciously prepared and commissioned for the leadership role they are going to have to fulfil. There is indeed a plan of salvation, and Luke shows it to us. The prodigal son is invited to return.

In a few minutes I shall be inviting the two Michaels, and by extension everyone present this evening, to receive a copy of St John's Gospel. John again is different, much more different than the others. People have argued and will go on arguing about precisely what John was aiming to do. But there is no doubt that here we have theology, profound theology, wrestling through story and symbol, through meditation on time and eternity, with an event of cosmic proportions which defies description. All the books in the world could not contain its full meaning. Yet it has to be expressed, however obliquely, in the thought forms of those who are to receive it. Here is the intellectual task of evangelism, a much needed one in our day, as we try to get to grips with a climate of thought which is in many ways radically different from that of the first century.

Four evangelists. Four different aims and styles. Inevitably I have had to spell out differences between them with crude brush strokes. My point is simply that, if in the first expressions of the gospel these differences were necessary, perhaps twenty centuries later two evangelists, however gifted, are not enough. Nor even two thousand. Perhaps the whole Church is needed to express the whole gospel. Perhaps all of us are the springboard whose energy God wants to use. And if that is so, then all of us in heart and mind must stand alongside the two Michaels as in God's name we go out together, diverse but united, to proclaim the Good News.

Eton's 550th Anniversary

Sermon in Eton College Chapel, 29 May 1990

This is where the College began – here in the Chapel. We can be thankful that Henry's original intention to make it larger than Salisbury Cathedral was never carried out. But it was the Chapel, large or not so large, which lay at the centre of his vision. There are many other contexts in which to celebrate the glories of Eton past and present. But they find their focus here in worship, because it was Henry's dearest wish that his future leaders in Church and state should be as devoted and upright as himself.

In fact walks to Windsor and chance meetings with the king

were an early feature of College life. We are told that he 'exhorted them to follow the paths of virtue, seasoning his advice with gifts of money'. He also advised them against visiting courtiers, 'lest they should come to a taste of their abandoned living'. Unfortunately, improving conversations with the monarch soon dropped out of the curriculum. And Henry's instructions on the appointment of staff – 'I would rather have them somewhat weak in music than defective in knowledge of the Scriptures' – now look somewhat less compelling.

Nevertheless, the basic religious orientation has remained. The tradition of worship has continued and flourished. And Henry's prayer of grateful acceptance of God's purpose for our lives has been engrained into the minds of all Etonians: 'Thou knowest what thou wouldst do with me; do with me according to thy will . . .'. Almost everything else has changed in five hundred and fifty years, but surely King Henry would recognize and rejoice in what we are doing now and count us as having been faithful to his vision.

Perhaps, though, not as faithful in all respects as he might have hoped. Etonians have shone in most walks of life, but the school has produced remarkably few church leaders. There was an undistinguished Archbishop of Canterbury in the eighteenth century, who was criticized for holding rowdy parties in Lambeth Palace. And there was a similarly undistinguished one in the nineteenth century, John Sumner, who for a time was an assistant master here, and hated it. He was known in school as 'Crumpet Sumner' on account of his complexion.

Archbishop William Temple as a young man, comparing Eton with Rugby, described Etonians as having 'an air of elegant indolence. No boy is so pleasant as the good sort of Etonian, but he is usually without much moral energy.'

That may have been true when Temple wrote it in 1916. I suspect that in the intervening years some of the moral energy has been coming back in the form of social conscience. I hope so, because cleverness, power, privilege, and consciousness of success, without moral energy are a dangerous combination. And an education which doesn't generate moral energy as it equips its pupils for leadership lacks the vital component.

But can we go further than this? What about piety and

devotion? This Chapel was built, not just to generate social conscience, but for prayer and worship, for devotion to God. And it is on this central feature of King Henry's intention that his own example is at its most ambivalent. Must humility and piety, gentleness and generosity of spirit, erode the will to rule? How does the kind of self-abnegation Henry saw as his Christian duty square with the decisiveness, craft, firmness of purpose and readiness to endure unpopularity, required of leaders? Must a strong Christian be a weak king?

In the long term, perhaps, it is his qualities as a man of God which shine out the more clearly, and whose fruits we enjoy today. The politics which seemed so important then, and which proved so disastrous for him, are dead and forgotten – except occasionally in Yorkshire. But *at the time*, piety and politics, sanctity and worldly success, were uncomfortable bedfellows. And Henry paid the price.

They are still uncomfortable bedfellows; not least in a school where many will expect to achieve worldly success of one kind or another, perhaps not as prime ministers these days, but as 'something in the city'. It is a school where the chances of exercising leadership are high, where we can rightly say that we have had the best which education can provide. The name Eton can still arouse envy or mockery among those who look at us as some kind of privileged élite. The task of taking hold of these perceptions, and bringing Christian understanding to bear on them, and trying to combine them with a genuine devotion to God, is by no means easy.

Perhaps this very act of thanksgiving can help to show us the way. The fact that we look back, not just fifty years, but five hundred and fifty, can bring home the point that most of what we now possess we have been given. Certainly there are achievements to celebrate, achievements within the recent past and achievements for which people now present are responsible. But our primary purpose is to show gratitude for what we have received. And the Christian word for that is grace.

Grace is about what we have been given without deserving. It is about the love of God which upholds us despite ourselves. It is about the faithfulness of God who will meet us in whatever success or failure lies ahead. It is about not taking things for granted, and being thankful. At the same time it is about being released from anxious self-concern, and set free.

What has all this to do with being an Etonian who wants somehow to combine piety and politics, sanctity and success? Who maybe has caught a glimpse here in this very place, as I did nearly fifty years ago, that life is edged around with transcendent mystery and that we can't be fully human until we respond to it?

An awareness of grace is a good place to start. I sometimes say to myself that the best part of being an Etonian is that you don't have to worry whether you are an Etonian or not. That is a paradoxical and absurdly élitist way of putting it. The point is that having received so much, and having learnt to be unself-consciously thankful for it, there is no need to go on and on about it. I see it as a parable in miniature of how an awareness of grace can set us free, free both from shame and disappoint-ment about the past, and free also from being smug and self-conscious about it.

It is a lesson which can be carried over into life, into whatever successes or failures come our way. Grace sets us free; free to be self-confident without being self-satisfied; free to love and pursue excellence without wanting to grab it all for ourselves; free to accept that we have been given great privileges and great responsibilities without making these into an excuse for superiority and pride; free to have, and not to have, because we enjoy what has been given to us without supposing that it is ours.

A life rooted in the grace of God is not only compatible with the world of politics, and business, and practical affairs, but essential to its health. Somehow good King Henry knew this. He began his prayer with the basis of it all, 'O Lord Jesus Christ who hast created and redeemed me . . .'.[1] But he couldn't quite put it into effect, except in founding colleges. And thus it was that he became a means of grace to us.

Note

1. The whole prayer, which is constantly used in this chapel, reads: 'O Lord Jesus Christ who hast created and redeemed me, and brought me to what I now am; thou knowest what thou wouldest do with me; do with me according to thy will; for thy tender mercy's sake.'

PART
5

On Being Liberal

_____ 16 _____

Reflections on the Liberal Position

From The Weight of Glory: Essays for Peter Baelz, *edited by D. W. Hardy and P. H. Sedgwick (T. & T. Clark 1991)*

Liberalism is a slippery concept. I doubt whether 'the liberal position', about which I have been asked to reflect, exists as such, or whether there is any one set of ideas or attitudes on which those who value the word 'liberal' would agree. It is best described in the lives of individuals. The wide range of topics discussed in this book conveys something of the breadth of interest, and the questioning, and the interplay between theology and secular concerns, which are characteristic of liberal spirits, and notably of Peter Baelz himself. But the notion, frequently canvassed these days, that there is a cohort of liberals within the Church of England who share certain definite aims and assumptions, and who consciously foster what has been called 'the liberal ascendency' seems to me to reveal a deep misunderstanding of the liberal phenomenon.

I intend therefore to start by describing two individuals, both of whom I had the good fortune to know in Cambridge at a formative period in my own life, and who were liberal in strikingly different ways.

To hear Charles Raven lecturing or preaching at the height of his powers was unforgettable. The sustained eloquence, the breadth of vision and knowledge, the sense of intellectual adventure, swept his audiences along, and Cambridge under-graduates in the immediate post-war years packed the lecture halls and churches to hear him, myself among them. In later years when he felt Cambridge had rejected him, as a lonely ex-Regius Professor of Divinity and ex-Vice-Chancellor demoted to being Warden of Madingley Hall, I came to know him personally, and found he could work the same magic in a room with half a dozen students. The last time I met him he came bounding up the stairs to my room, apologizing for being late because he had had a heart attack that morning.

This larger-than-life quality infused all his teaching. He was at his most impressive in talking about science and religion, and in particular in his exposition of the seventeeth-century Cambridge Platonists. The first volume of his now largely forgotten Gifford lectures, *Natural Religion and Christian Theology* (1953), is a valuable historical summary telling the story of science and religion, unusually, from the perspective of natural history rather than physics. But the second volume which attempts a synthesis between religious experience and a scientific world-view reveals serious weaknesses, both scientific and theological.

Despite his strong advocacy of science and scientific ways of thinking, there were occasions, particularly in his account of evolution, when he abandoned them. Ill-defined claims about the work of God's Spirit substituted for scientific explanations, and left him vulnerable to advances in knowledge. I remember feeling uneasy when listening to him expatiate in his lectures on the inexplicability of the evolution of the cuckoo,[1] and in this respect, as in others, time has passed him by. Theologically, too, despite current enthusiasm in some quarters about the work of the Spirit, it is easy to see the weakness of a theology of nature in which the Spirit is identified with more or less everything that is going on. In Daniel Jenkins' words, Dr Raven's 'diffused world-spirit manifesting itself everywhere with large-hearted comprehensiveness' is 'like a sign-post pointing in all directions and therefore giving no guidance at all'.[2] In the 1990s some eyebrows would also doubtless be raised about a Christology based on Christ's power 'to awaken and quicken our sensitiveness . . . All else, the works of power, the fulfilment of prophecies, the Virgin birth, the physical resurrection, are no doubt appropriate but surely secondary;

and if the evidence for them does not convince us, we need not therefore feel that we are outcast from Christendom'.[3]

This was a liberalism rooted in a major attempt at synthesis. The vision was there, a vision of a religio-scientific world brought together in at least a provisional harmony. Teilhard de Chardin's numerous books expressed a similar, and more widely acknowledged, vision when they began to be published a few years later. But in both Raven and Teilhard the synthesis involved some cutting of the corners; their theologies avoided the awkward questions being raised by neo-orthodoxy about the particularity of Christ, and sin, and human limitations, and their science tended to lapse into vagueness at crucial moments. Teilhard was unfortunately never criticized in his lifetime. Raven, as I knew him, was better at talking than listening. It was said of him, perhaps unkindly, that 'he did not become the leader he might have been because of his utter inability to absorb or relate himself to a contrary idea'.[4]

Alec Vidler is a liberal in a totally different tradition. He prefers the word 'liberality' with its suggestion that what is at stake is an attitude of mind, rather than some grand synthesis, or party, or identifiable tradition. It is significant that the title of the book for which he is most likely to be remembered is *Soundings*, and his theological hero is F. D. Maurice, who described himself as 'only a digger'.

I was fortunate in being able to watch Alec Vidler at work over a number of years as a member of an informal group which advised him in his work as Editor of *Theology*. There was the same breadth of interest as in Raven, the same impatience with what he saw as narrow-minded ecclesiasticism, but a historian's suspicion of extravagant claims and over-simple answers. He has described his work in this context as 'theological midwifery'. The fact that *Theology* under his editorship hardly ever carried editorials is further evidence of his desire not to pursue a particular line, but to encourage exploration. He wrote of himself, 'I remember that in the early years of my editorship some readers used to complain that they could not make out what *Theology* now stood for: and I took this as a compliment rather than the reverse!'[5]

In a different context, writing about the New Testament character possessed by a 'legion' of devils, he spelt out the dividedness of the digging, as opposed to the synthesizing, liberal:

> I allow that in the end a man needs to be one, unified, just as mankind does. But *in the end*. Is this what the theologians, with their inelegant jargon, call an eschatological possibility or promise?
>
> But on the way to the end it may be better to be more than one man, pulled this way and that, with plenty of discords and jagged edges, trailing uncertainties, with clashing loyalties, ever and again amazed and perplexed and tongue-tied. Perhaps again this is why theologians have had so much to say about being justified by *faith*, for faith, unlike sight, stammers and is dumb.[6]

Soundings tried to convey something of this attitude in a time of theological complacency. Biblical theology ruled the roost. Theological questions were to be answered by careful study of the language of the Bible. Questions which fell outside this narrow circle of interest could safely be ignored. Vidler wrote in his introduction: 'We believe that there are very important questions which theologians are now being called upon to face, and which are not yet being faced with the necessary seriousness and determination.'[7]

The impetus came from a group of Cambridge theologians, and once again Vidler acted as midwife. I was invited to join the group in 1960 for a crucial meeting at Launde Abbey where the decision was made to produce a volume of essays. These became the first public stirrings of the theological revolution which was to overtake the Churches in the decade which followed. In terms of publicity *Soundings* was soon swamped by John Robinson's *Honest to God*, and members of the group reflected wryly that John Robinson had not been invited to join it on the grounds that he was too firmly wedded to Biblical Theology – as many of his subsequent writings demonstrated.

Predictably the main public interest in *Soundings* centred on the essay by Harry Williams which was a plea to take seriously the insights of Freud, and which interestingly began with a dismissal of Raven's attack on Freud in his Gifford lectures. What set the correspondents buzzing, though, was a hint that in certain psychological circumstances fornication might be appropriate and right, and that what prevented it was not morality but fear. The suggestion was made in very modest terms, but with hindsight it can be seen as a prelude to the sexual revolution of the sixties. Most of the other authors of *Soundings*, including Vidler himself, had grave doubts about whether the essay should be published. In the end Harry Williams' argument prevailed on the ground that he was being honest to his own experience and that of the authors he was quoting. What claim could the book make to be an honest exploration of contemporary issues if it were censored at this vital point? But here we run straight into a typical liberal dilemma. How far can honesty be taken before it becomes destructive of confidence in those who pursue it?

Vidler's own concern was to bring theology out of its intellectual ghetto. 'When theologians are on speaking terms only with themselves they are doomed to frustration and indeed to damnation',[8] was his way of putting it. But taking theology out of the divinity schools also entails risks, risks to which Raven exposed himself only too obviously by trying to Christianize a broad sweep of secular knowledge. Vidler's strategy was to use secular methods of criticism, but to hide his own faith under a veil of theological inscrutability, which during his time as Dean of King's teased and fascinated his fellow dons. 'If we must have preachers,' he said in his final Cambridge sermon, 'I like them to be oblique and reserved and even enigmatic.'[9]

He tells the story of how on his arrival at King's as its Dean, and finding himself responsible for college discipline, he went round the walls of the college directing that the spikes and broken glass on top of them should be removed. In a sense he has been doing that all his life: not underestimating the importance of limits, but making it easier to move in and out by unorthodox routes. His ministry as a 'theological midwife' rested on his historian's sense of the survivability of Christianity even through tumultuous change, and his conviction as a critic that the only way to knowledge is through open enquiry. As David Edwards said of him on his retirement in 1964, he saved the Church of England from stagnation.

I have chosen to concentrate on these two men from an age now vanished, partly because Peter Baelz was himself in Cambridge not long after their heyday, and more particularly because a little historical distance can help us to take a cooler look at contemporary controversies. I am not an historian, and feel safer in writing of things I know at first hand.

Ian Ramsey was yet another kind of liberal, driven by his need to come to terms with the Oxford philosophy of his day. His elaborate recastings of Christian theology, his insistence that all theological language can do is to provide models pointing towards a disclosure of God, and his rather elusive thoughts about the extent to which these models are rooted in empirical reality, would surely have made him an object of much suspicion in the nineteen-eighties. Yet he went to Durham, revered as its bishop, and hailed as the brightest intellectual light in the Church of England. How, I wonder, would he have reacted to today's controversies? And, more to the point, was there a fundamental difference in degree between his liberalism and that of David Jenkins who followed him to Durham eleven years after his death?

A constant feature of liberalism is the wish to take seriously the intellectual climate in which faith has to be lived. This is not the same as following intellectual fashion. At the frontiers of academic conversation there obviously has to be an engagement with ideas which are currently in vogue. Much theological writing at this level, like any other writing, tends to be ephemeral and is only dangerously misleading if it is assumed at that instant to express the faith of the Church. But underneath such temporary eddies there are much more enduring ground swells, perhaps even permanent alterations in human consciousness and perceptions. These are not mere matters for fashionable intellectual debate. In the long term they affect everybody. And the hard question which has to be answered by theologians is how far these ought to shape theological development.

Serious liberalism does not start reconstructing its theology at the first hint of secular change. Nor is it wise, in my view, to be too busy with reconstruction à la Raven even when so-called modern knowledge seems well established. But it needs to take seriously the questions posed by fundamental sea-changes, and to be ready to live with loose ends, partial insights, and a measure of agnosticism, without losing its grip on the essentials of faith.

What are these long-term changes? The development of

science and the broad understanding of the nature of the universe it has given us is one of them. A sense of historical perspective often manifesting itself in terms of historical relativism is another. The discovery of hitherto unknown depths in the human psyche is a third. It would not be hard to list others.

All of these can be, and have been, attacked. There are fashionable attacks on science, for instance, on the grounds of its reductionism and in the name of various kinds of holism. There is a general critique of the Enlightenment which has exposed the shaky philosophical foundations of many of the more extreme claims made on behalf of science. Theological liberalism has no vested interest in ignoring these attacks. But it has to ask whether they place serious question marks over prevailing secular orthodoxies, or whether they simply represent marginal adjustments to a major intellectual construction which will easily survive them.

My own view is that the changes scientific discoveries, for instance, have made to our perception of the world are so firmly based, so deeply rooted in modern Western consciousness, and so bound up with our way of life, that Christians ignore them at their peril. I can give a rather extreme example of this by quoting a letter I received recently after speaking in Parliament on embryo research. I had been making the point that the development of individual lives is as gradual, and as obscure, as the transition from hominid to human in the course of evolution. The letter was signed in his official capacity by the secretary of a reputable organization sponsored by 27 MPs, and the first part of it read as follows:

> Thank you for so clearly stating in the House of Lords what many of us had suspected, namely, that you are not a Christian. This is particularly helpful for those of us who are concerned about who should become the next Primate within the Anglican Church.
>
> If the report is correct, during the discussion on the Embryology Bill you said that 'Christians are not required to believe in the historical existence of Adam and Eve.' Furthermore, you evidently went on to subscribe to the completely unproven and indeed even scientifically unsound theory of evolution.

One wonders what other parts of the Bible you do not believe.

There are several points of interest here. The first is the definition of 'Christian' by reference to a particular moral judgement which historically has never before carried this weight or even been generally agreed. The second is the linking of that judgement to particular historical claims about the Bible which were in principle set aside by most theologians more than a century ago. The third, and most revealing, is the claim to have scientific evidence to support a face-value interpretation of the biblical story. Science, in other words, is not set on one side. It is used selectively to bolster a theological position which seems weak if held on purely theological grounds.

This kind of argument, based on naive fundamentalism and suitably doctored science, is only beginning to make inroads into Britain, but is already a serious threat to orthodox science and scientifically informed theology in the USA. Liberals of whatever kind may find themselves fighting in such circumstances, not only for the intellectual integrity of theology, but also for the integrity of science. The whole exercise is richly paradoxical. A travesty of science is used in argument against mainline scientific theories, thereby unconsciously revealing the extent to which the power and prestige of science are now accepted even by those who for theological reasons want to reject some of its findings. This has nothing to do with the normal process whereby scientific theories are constantly criticized and sometimes overthrown. It has everything to do with the desire to use science for one's own purposes. Theologians need to be alert to the difference, and this is a yet further reason for taking science seriously.

In gentler academic climates the difficulties may be greater, because the frontiers are more blurred and the influence of new knowledge on theological understanding more subtle. Away from the battle lines drawn between various kinds of dogmatic conservatism, whether religious or secular, it is hard to know how much new knowledge can be absorbed by a traditional faith without turning it into something else. What are the essentials of faith on which believers have to maintain their grip while accepting criticism and allowing a measure of agnosticism? If Adam and Eve belong to the margins of theology, and if nothing essential is lost by treating their story as non-historical myth, can the same be said of the various stories of the resurrection?

As recent events have proved, such questions can appear highly threatening, even when every allowance is made for the different historical, scientific and literary provenances of the two kinds of stories. But it is worth noting how the most perceptive liberal theologians, Ian Ramsey for instance, have treated the oddities in the resurrection stories, not as a basis for making negative historical judgements, but as pointers to their transcendent meaning. We don't understand anything about the resurrection at all unless we see them, not just as narrative, but as stories which make an overwhelming claim on us and which disclose God by their very oddness.[10]

Perhaps the safest guideline in this difficult territory is the belief that the readiness to receive new truth itself belongs to the essence of faith. F. J. A. Hort, the least well-known of the famous nineteenth-century trio Lightfoot, Westcott and Hort, made this point memorably in his lecture, 'Christ – The Truth':

> It is not too much to say that the Gospel itself can never be fully known till nature as well as man is fully known; and that the manifestation of nature as well as man in Christ is part of his manifestation of God. As the Gospel is the perfect introduction to all truth, so on the other hand it is itself known only in proportion as it is used for the enlightenment of departments of truth which seem at first sight to be beyond its boundaries . . . 'I am the Truth' . . . marks every truth which seems alien to Christ as a sign that the time is come for better knowledge of Christ, since no truth can be alien to him who is the Truth.[11]

The search for truth, in other words, through rational critical understanding (which needs of course to be self-critical as well) has theological roots no less significant than the theological basis of revelation. Both are from God: in different modes and degrees, maybe, but both originating and finding their fulfilment in him. It is this kind of faith, I believe, which undergirds the best liberal approaches to theology. I want to emphasize that this is a theological undergirding, not an absence of faith in God, but a conviction that he is to be found wherever the human mind can reach.

This is why the equation of liberalism with lack of faith is frequently so wide of the mark. I cannot speak for all liberals because, as I have tried to show, liberalism is a complex phenomenon and I approach it from its conservative rather than from its radical side. But from my perspective an intoxication with the greatness and the mystery of God lies at the heart of it.

I end with a brief mention of so-called 'liberal causes'. Raven pursued some, notably pacifism and feminism. Vidler didn't, unless it was the constant defence of academic freedom. Theological liberals in our own day are accused of knee-jerk reactions on a variety of fashionable issues. But I am not sure matters are as simple as this. Pacifism, for instance, does not seem to me to be characteristically liberal. On the contrary, it is frequently grounded in moral absolutism and a refusal to learn the lessons of history. Other forms of adherence to causes, whether liberal or conservative, owe more to political than to theological orientation. Other causes, and these are perhaps the only ones which belong truly within a liberal tradition of theology as I have described it, emerge from new facts, or new interpretations of old facts, or a new willingness to face facts which have hitherto been ignored. Agonizing over such issues as homosexuality belongs here. But the idea that, because somebody adopts a liberal attitude in some matters, he or she must be liberal in everything, seems to me to be plainly untrue.

There is, in short, no identikit for being a liberal. It is possible to recognize, however, some whose lives have clearly been shaped by the gracious liberality of God, and who display its marks in their own liberality towards all that God has made. These are lives for which both Church and world can rightly give thanks.

Notes

1. See, for example, *Natural Religion and Christian Theology*, vol. 2 (Cambridge University Press 1953), pp. 137ff.
2. Quoted in F. W. Dillistone, *Charles Raven* (Hodder & Stoughton 1975), pp. 287f.

 3. *Natural Religion*, vol. 2, p. 80.
 4. Dillistone, p. 415.
 5. Quoted by D. L. Edwards in *Theology* (January 1965), p. 7.
 6. A. R. Vidler, *Scenes from Clerical Life* (Collins 1977), p. 172.
 7. *Soundings*, ed. A. R. Vidler (Cambridge University Press 1962), p. xi.
 8. Vidler (1977), p. 177.
 9. ibid., p. 169.
10. See, for example, I. T. Ramsey, *Religious Language* (SCM Press 1957), p. 127ff.
11. F. J. A. Hort, *The Way The Truth The Life* (Macmillan 1894²), pp. 83, 85.

17

Rationality and Truth

Article in The Independent, *5 January 1991*

There is a dilemma at the heart of religious truth–claims, which needs to be faced if the Churches, now launched into the Decade of Evangelism, are to break free from their damaging internecine disputes. Disagreements between so-called traditionalists and so-called liberals continue to rankle, and those who enjoy stirring the pot speak darkly of conspiracies. Energy which might be channelled into persuading an unbelieving world to accept the Christian faith, is siphoned off into internal struggles, all because the battleground is wrongly perceived.

The dilemma which sets these opposing forces in action is that religious truth must in some sense come from God if it is to be more than a reflection of our own hopes, wishes and prejudices; yet how can it be known that it does indeed come from God unless it can in some sense be subject to rational scrutiny?

There are plenty of refinements on this dilemma. The word 'rational', for instance, is not as self-evident as it seems, and there are good grounds for saying that our Western tradition of rational argument is rooted in our history, including our Christian history, rather than in some absolute principle. Conversely, the claim that faith in God's self-revelation can provide an unassailable basis for truth, has to reckon with the fact that there are competing claims to such self-revelation, and competing interpretations of what has been revealed. Furthermore, truth itself is a slippery word, especially when applied to realities which transcend definition.

Setting aside such refinements, however, let me concentrate on one form in which the dilemma presents itself to those who would be Christian evangelists or apologists. The two titles themselves point to the two sides of it. Are we to argue? Or simply to proclaim?

St Paul at first sight seems in no doubt. The first three chapters of 1 Corinthians, with their ringing condemnation of mere human wisdom, provide the perfect text for Christian believers who wish to assert the limitations of rationality. If 'God has made the wisdom of this world look foolish', and if it is not the clever but the weak and powerless who are called to faith, then it would seem to follow that the search for truth in the light of human reasoning is doomed to failure. Pure naked faith is all that is needed. Tertullian was right: 'I believe because it is impossible'. The true believer has the perfect answer to criticism. Anything can be believed because God by definition can do anything, and reasons suggesting that he might not have done so can be ruled out of court as the misapprehensions of faithless minds.

Is this what St Paul actually meant? I doubt it, if we are to take seriously the amount of reasoned discussion elsewhere in his letters. It is true that there is a famous passage in Romans (11.33–6) where at the end of elaborate argument about predestination which is clearly getting into great difficulties, he slips away from it into a little hymn on the wisdom and inscrutability of God. But as a brilliant theological innovator he can hardly have discounted the powers of mind which made him so formidable.

The key to his disparagement of wisdom surely lies, not in a rejection of rational argument as such, but in the inability of the human mind to grasp through its own resources the central mystery of Christ's cross. Salvation is not by knowledge, and in particular not by the kind of Gnosticism with which the early Church had to contend, but by faith. Our acceptance by God is rooted in what God himself has done, and not in what we, with our human self-centredness, may think or decide.

There is a self-regarding wisdom, a wisdom distorted by human limitations, which is always liable and ready to create God in its own image.

All this we may concede. Christian faith transcends wisdom. It is not about adherence to a set of ideas clearly defined within the compass of human thought, but about allegiance to a person who remains ultimately mysterious. Rational thought about the person of Christ dissolves into a set of paradoxes which serve only to safeguard the mystery. And the mystery itself is made still more inaccessible to us by its particularity and contingency. A single human life, a single set of historical events, bear the weight of eternal truth. 'What think ye of Christ?' is both the starting-point and the irreducible test of faith.

None of this, however, has prevented Christians from trying to use their minds in spelling out the significance of these central claims and relating them to other forms of knowledge. How this is to be done and how far it can be taken is, as I see it, a main bone of contention between traditionalists and liberals. There is a whole spectrum of responses from a glorying in irrationalism at one extreme to reductionist attempts to 'explain' Christ at the other. But the real conversations ought to be going on between those Christians, and surely they are the vast majority, who are unwilling either to lose the mystery of Christ or to circumvent the exceedingly difficult historical and philosophical questions which it poses.

A historical faith is vulnerable to historical investigation. It may conversely challenge assumptions about what is significant in history and about ways in which the past can still be a living force in the present. There is a sheer givenness about the New Testament which no amount of historical analysis can take away. But it is quite compatible with belief in the divine mystery of Christ to hold that a huge number of historical questions about the actual life of Jesus are likely to remain forever unresolved.

Similarly, while it is vital to grasp that God is not a philosophical construct arrived at by a process of reasoning, nevertheless there is an obligation on those who try to think philosophically to make some sense of their religious claims. What goes on in fact is a process of internal dialogue, a to-ing and fro-ing between the raw experience of faith and rational understanding. Like historical analysis, it is a process which is never finished. But out of it there develop traditions of workable concepts and significant connections which stand the test of time, and which manage to point to that which transcends them without it being reduced to human dimensions.

Truth is not circumscribed by rationality, but it needs rationality to know itself as truth. I wonder if it is too much to hope that Christians who in the past have been adamant in disagreeing with one another, may begin to perceive an agenda here on which it is possible to work together.

18

Surprised by Hell

Article in The Independent, *15 July 1991*

Hell is full of surprises. I am not just thinking of the obvious sense in which the surprised goats of Matthew 25.44 wondered what they had done to deserve their fate. The surprises I have in mind spring from a more mundane judgement, in fact from judgement on a modest essay on hell I wrote last month for my diocesan newspaper.

A correspondent had asked me for an article because one of the damaging experiences of his youth had been the teaching of the sect to which he then belonged, that 'eternal conscious punishment was for all unbelievers'. Subsequently I had an even more powerful letter from a mother whose distressed daughter-in-law had been told by her clergyman that her stillborn child must inevitably go to hell for eternity because it was unbaptized. How such teaching could possibly be compatible with belief in the love of God, and how the idea of eternal punishment unrelieved by any change of mind could possibly be conceived as just, are questions which demand an answer, no matter how strongly some passages of Scripture speak of an eternal divide between the saved and the lost.

As the Churches put evangelism higher on their agendas, there is also a need to think more clearly about the motive for it. Do present-day Christians really believe, as many of our forebears undoubtedly did, that all unevangelized souls go straight to hell? Or is it more true to say that goodness forced on people under threat of torture is not goodness at all? that the motive for evangelism must be love not fear?

In my essay I also referred to the familiar point that some of the more lurid descriptions of burning fires and undying worms in the New Testament were imagery, now known to refer to the Jerusalem rubbish dump (Gehenna), and were not to be taken literally. Traditional pictures of hell owe more to mistranslations, to later interpretations, to medieval excesses, to poets like Dante and Milton, and above all to the failure to grasp the full implications of salvation, than to the original Scriptures and to early Christian teaching.

But I was careful to point out that to criticize the idea of hell on ethical grounds, and to reinterpret New Testament symbolism, is not in any way to abandon the belief that actions can have eternal consequences. In fact hell is a profound symbol of the seriousness of moral choices, and of the irreducible character of human freedom.

One way of reconciling these opposites is to say that we create hell for ourselves. It is not an objective reality, not a place or state created by God as a means of executing his justice, but is the way we experience self-absorption, despair, and unwillingness to open ourselves to his love. Heaven, by contrast, is not self-created but is the God-given fulfilment of all his intentions for us. There is therefore a real lostness from which we need to be rescued. But it is not a lostness imposed upon us by God as a punishment, and therefore raises no question about God's moral goodness or his love towards us.

I had thought that these were present-day theological platitudes. Hence the surprise when sections of the media went berserk. Everybody wanted interviews. I was even invited to appear on Newsnight. A national daily claimed that its readers had a particular interest in hell, and then produced both a leading article and an item in its gossip column. The editorial contained a curious reference to the idea of a 'physical hell', thereby subscribing to the double error of supposing that anything which is not physical is not objective, and anything which is not objective is not real. For all its pious tone it was peddling old-fashioned materialism. Another newspaper fell into the same trap the other way round, in supposing that if hell is self-created it must be 'all in the mind', and to that extent unreal and insignificant. Both showed an alarming incapacity to handle the notions of spiritual reality, the inner reality of persons, and by implication the reality of God. Part of the evangelistic task of Christians, therefore, must be to rehabilitate the language in which such matters may be sensibly discussed.

A small army of correspondents divided themselves between appreciation and denunciation, some of the latter showing a particular interest in my own ultimate fate. Critics on the whole were content to quote a few predictable texts from the Bible as if these settled the matter. Most seemed unaware that, even if one takes every word of the Bible at its face value, there is still theological work to be done in translating the wide variety of biblical teaching into comprehensible and consistent doctrines. Too many people seem stuck with a stark either/or alternative – between either simply repeating biblical phrases as if these answered all the questions, or creating one's own belief more or less regardless of the Bible. Letter after letter which comes through my post simply assumes that these are the alternatives. Somehow we need to escape from this kind of sterile confrontation, whether between fundamentalists and liberals, self-styled 'Biblical Christians' or 'non-Biblical Christians' – whatever they might be – and acknowledge that we are all trying to take the Bible seriously.

One of the difficulties in interpreting the Bible lies in the fact that different bits of it say different things. Hell is a good example. There are undoubtedly some very direct and terrifying statements. But there are also plenty of passages with a picture of the end as a gathering up of the whole created order in Christ. Furthermore, there are insights into the nature of God derived from the whole story of Christ's death and resurrection and the promise of forgiveness – insights which seem to make the idea of everlasting punishment incompatible with the main thrust of the gospel. The biblical interpreter has to make sense of all this, and more, not because he or she is liberal or conservative, modern or traditionalist, but because the questions are there in the Bible itself.

The violence, not to say the virulence, of the things some people say about hell, points to a strong desire to punish and reject. A. N. Wilson in his much-publicized conversion away from Christianity seems to have discovered – rather late – that religion can be dangerous. It can arouse some quite ugly passions. And sometimes the more deeply people feel themselves to be committed, the more ready they are to exclude and condemn those who fail to measure up to their own way of seeing things. Talk of hell can touch the hellish impulses inside each of us. All of which is another reason for trying to look coolly at what it means.

This is even more important at a time when the upsurge of traditionalist religion can threaten to bring back unwelcome fears and hatreds alongside more desirable emphases. There is a proper fear of God, a proper awe in the face of his holiness. We need to recognize the dangers of self-centredness, faithlessness and despair. But the paralysing fear of punishment which dogged some earlier Christian generations, has, I believe, no place in the Christian gospel. James Joyce in revolting as a young man against the famous Jesuit sermon on hell was surely wiser than his teachers.

19

Living With Other Faiths

Diocesan Newspaper, May 1992

On the first day of our first term new undergraduates in my College used to meet the Provost – the Head of the College – in his drawing room. We stood there, a nervous circle of a hundred or so young men, while he greeted each of us in turn.

'Well my boy, which school do you come from?'
'Puddlewick School, Sir.'
'Best school in the world. Bless you.'

. . . and so on round the room.

Some years later, when I knew him better, I tackled him on this performance: 'How can you say that each school is the best school in the world?'

He looked at me and chuckled: 'Did you have a mother? Wasn't she the best mother in the world?'

It was a disgraceful piece of relativism, an assessment of each school and each mother simply from the point of view of the person most concerned. We know in fact that some schools are better than others, just as some mothers are better than others. Truth in such matters is not merely what is true for us, or true from our perspective.

Yet the Provost had a point. We value what we know best. Knowing is inseparable from loving. And loving requires involvement. So although it is possible, and sometimes necessary, to make comparisons on a more or less objective scale – examination results, or Brownie points for mothers, for example – there are elements in our knowledge of institutions, and relationships, and human experience in general, which cannot be treated in this way. Belonging to something or somebody contains elements which those who stand outside this experience can never fully understand.

This is one reason why dialogue between people of different religious faiths is so difficult and can arouse such misgivings. For many people their faith is both their school and their mother. It is natural, and in some circumstances essential, to make claims that one's faith is the best in the world, based on the only authentic God-given revelation, and thus not strictly comparable to other faith claims. To suppose otherwise would be to slide down the slippery slope of relativism, being nice to everyone for the sake of making them feel at ease. Dialogue thus seems caught between an unprincipled blessing of differences on the one hand, and on the other the assertion of incompatible claims with each side believing that its own truth must prevail.

These two stereotypes of dialogue constantly recur in popular presentations of inter-faith issues, and both can be highly damaging. A freewheeling relativism cuts out the heart of Christianity – belief in the unique person and work of Christ. A hard-nosed exclusivism devalues the experience of those who differ from us, ignoring the fact that truth has to be known from the inside, not merely judged from a distance.

Much Christian effort has been put into seeking a course to steer between these two approaches. The Bible, confusingly, appears to lend some support to both of them. 'He that is not with me is against me' (Luke 11.23) has to be set alongside, 'He that is not against you is for you' (Luke 9.50). Much of the Bible story centres on the chosen people of God. Yet both Old and New Testaments, and especially St Mark's Gospel, go out of their way to stress the part played by outsiders in the discernment of faith and the education of God's people. Dialogue, in other words, is not a fashionable new device imposed on biblical religion; it is inherent in the process of biblical revelation.

How then can we hold fast to Christian truth while

respecting, and being ready to learn from, the faith of others? Broadly speaking four ways of squaring this particular circle have been proposed:

1. All religions are attempts to express the same ultimate truths – all roads lead to God.

2. Religions are complex social systems which give us different, but complementary, pictures of ultimate reality. The differences between them are real, and they need each other for a fuller apprehension of the truth.

3. Christ is the ultimate revelation of God, but other faiths may have seen something of Christ, so that what is true in them will ultimately be seen to be related to him.

4. We simply do not know how faiths relate to one another, but if we remain faithful to what we have received and open to the experience of others, we believe we shall in the long run find meeting points where there can be mutual enrichment.

These four ways shade into one another, and none is entirely satisfactory. The first is too crude and ignores real differences. The second goes too far in the direction of relativism. The third can swing too far in the opposite direction, and members of other faiths may rightly resent being treated as if they were anonymous Christians. The fourth seems too vague, setting an agenda for dialogue without any idea of where it might lead. But at least it is honest in acknowledging that the dilemmas are not easily resolved. Actual inter-faith dialogue tends to make use of insights from all four.

The Provost at least got one point right. Our first need is to value what we have, without setting up artificial barriers against those whose background and experiences are different. But then we need to find delight in the faith of others without feeling threatened by it, or that we have to judge it, or subvert it. Our best Christian witness lies in our love for Christ and in the Christian quality of our lives. Our third need, as it was for those first-year undergraduates, is for space and time to explore the rich diversity of human life and belief, without trying to force it into the narrow mould of our own thinking.

Wise discrimination develops later. The truths which

endure begin to be distinguished from the finery in which they are clothed. Spirit speaks to spirit. And without knowing the end of the journey we may begin to see glimpses in each other's experience of the way, the truth and the life.

Epilogue

Ten Years as Archbishop

Robert Runcie had no hesitation about turning down the Archbishopric of York when it was offered to him in 1974. Nor, so Margaret Duggan tells us, had two other unnamed bishops who were offered it before him.[1] When, next time round in 1983, the invitation arrived on my desk, I accepted it straightaway. As Bishop of Durham I had already seen much of what the role entailed at close quarters, and was convinced of its potential. In fact much had happened between 1974 and 1983 to give it a new strategic significance.

Towards the end of Donald Coggan's time at Canterbury the small group of senior bishops, of whom I was one, met to consider a job specification for the next Archbishop of Canterbury, and to identify ways in which his intolerable load could be lightened. One obvious means was to develop a greater degree of partnership between the two archbishops and more sharing of responsibilities. The start of Synodical government in 1970 had dramatically reduced the significance of the separate Provinces, and the designation of the two archbishops as joint Presidents of the Synod had already indicated the kind of relationship expected of them. It seemed to me in 1983 that the time was ripe for a much more vigorous expression of this relationship, and that the different backgrounds, personalities and interests of Robert Runcie and myself could make it a potentially fruitful one.

How well it worked only history can tell. Robert Runcie and myself have been criticised for being too much alike, and too heavily committed to the so-called 'liberal establishment'. From within, our partnership felt very different. His style was cautious, intuitive, historically conscious, magisterial, with meticulous attention paid to presentation. Mine has been more pragmatic, readier to take swift decisions, more consciously geared to contemporary intellectual conflicts, and less urbane. In debate he was best at the broad comprehensive statement of general principle. My own role was frequently to enter debates near the end, usually with an unprepared speech, in order to act as sweeper-up. In committee he was perceptive in sensing when a proposal was not quite right in that it offended against some general principle. I saw my own contribution as trying to master the detail, and to offer practical solutions. He gave a huge amount of time to the Anglican Communion, an investment which paid off handsomely at the 1988 Lambeth Conference. My own major commitment was to ecumenism, both nationally and within the World Council of Churches. His social links were with the world of business and politics, and his great gifts of friendship gave him access to and knowledge of people across a very wide spectrum. My own concerns have been more academic, more centred on the world of ideas. We frequently consulted together on major issues. In short, I believe there was a genuine and helpful complementarity in our respective roles; and I suspect, though I have not the evidence to prove this, that we worked more closely together than the vast majority of our predecessors.

With a change of personalities the details are different but the co-operation continues. The leadership of the Church of England is a shared task. Although the Archbishop of Canterbury must inevitably attract the lion's share of public attention, close collaboration between the two Archbishops is a practical necessity. It also accords well with the characteristic Anglican understanding of authority as dispersed, rather than as concentrated in a single authoritative figure. This relationship, therefore, forms the essential background to what a present-day Archbishop of York must be and do. It must be assumed in what I now say about a few of those matters with which I have been particularly and personally involved.

Soon after my appointment I invited my fellow bishops in the North to tell me what they expected of an Archbishop. 'We want you to think,' was the answer which stuck most clearly in my mind. Among the huge amount of time spent overseeing a large diocese, keeping contact with other dioceses, fulfilling national and international responsibilities, trying to think has been one of my main concerns. Serious academic work is not possible; other demands fragment one's time and energies too much to allow the necessary concentration. My method has been to enter as sympathetically as I can into the particular issues faced by a wide variety of interest groups, and to tease out from within them where they seem to touch on some fundamental Christian insight. Much of the material in this book illustrates this approach.

At times it can seem dangerously secular. Many Christians suppose, wrongly in my view, that there is or ought to be a specifically Christian 'answer' to all the world's problems. In the general sense that all human concerns ultimately reach out towards God as their source and goal, one can claim that Christian faith has a bearing on everything. But in more immediate practical terms it is simply not true that there is a 'biblical' way of tackling issues, as if the insights and thought-forms of a previous age could be applied in a relatively unsophisticated way to matters of which the writers of the Bible were totally unaware. In consequence I find much contemporary Christian discussion of ethics and politics depressingly shallow. St Paul, by contrast had no compunction about using the secular morality of his day. In quoting secular moral codes and lists of qualities, as he frequently did, he set them in a theological context.[2] They were to be observed by those who had been set free through grace to live lives of holiness. But the actual content of the codes formed part of common morality.

Christian faith, in other words, provides the context, the motivation, the illumination, and at times the heroic challenge, but it does not require the abandonment of genuine secular insights, common sense, and ordinary powers of analysis. Christian thought has to be incarnated in the world of ordinary thought, and it is seldom clear precisely where one begins and the other ends. In the House of Lords debate on *in vitro* fertilization, for example, it seemed to me irresponsible to ignore the complex scientific evidence about the highly fluid process by which the identity of an embryo gradually develops. I was not therefore content to build an ethical policy on the easily disputable claim that personal identity begins at fertilization. I saw it as even less responsible to try to settle the matter by reference to the virginal conception of Jesus, as if a story told in Scripture to point to the mystery of Christ's origins could be used to give a definitive answer to a question which could not have been asked at all before the advent of modern embryology. But this scepticism about direct attempts to derive a specifically Christian answer in no way detracts from a proper Christian concern about the value and dignity of human life, even in its weakest and most vulnerable forms, or from Christian sensitivity towards the God-givenness of such life. The wonder experienced by any scientist in face of the mystery of life shades into that special kind of protectiveness felt by those who see in it evidences of God's glory.[3]

This, then, has been my general approach. As Moderator of the Church and Society Sub-Unit of the World Council of Churches from 1983 to 1991 I was involved at world level in planning a variety of projects, all aimed in some way to help local Christian communities to tackle issues raised by scientific and technological development.[4]

In Central America and South East Asia, for example, groups of scientists were encouraged to work with local church people on the subject of deforestation. In the Marshall Islands we were able to focus public attention on the long-term social effects of nuclear testing. For a time we worked with the World Health Organization on AIDS, and in 1988 I had to face an audience of African church leaders to try to persuade them, in the face of considerable resistance, that AIDS was not just a special problem for Western homosexuals, but was of vital concern in their own countries. In the Soviet Union we discussed with Russian Orthodox theologians their understanding of the uniqueness of human life, as made in the image of God, and the significance of this understanding in the way we should treat animals.

Towards the end much of my work with the WCC had to be focused on the Justice Peace and Integrity of Creation programme (JPIC) which was due to reach a climax in a World Convocation in Seoul in 1990. At the WCC Central Committee meeting in 1988 I tried unsuccessfully to abort plans for the Convocation and replace it by a much smaller working group, in the hope that this might produce some ideas of real intellectual and practical worth. But for political reasons change was impossible. The Koreans wanted a large prestigious world event to compensate them for losing out to Canberra in hosting the 1991 WCC Assembly. The Germans, in whose country we were meeting, were enthusiastic about JPIC and optimistic about the prospects of persuading everyone else to covenant with them on specific issues of world social policy. In the event the Convocation took place on the basis of ill-prepared and tendentious documentation. The rest of the world came with their own incompatible agendas. And the result was a rhetorical report full of high-sounding but impracticable aspirations, which had scarcely been discussed by the participants.

Since retiring from the WCC I have been chairman of a small group, mostly composed of similarly retired old hands in ecumenical work, who have tried to analyse why the WCC has suffered such a disastrous loss of credibility among opinion formers in the Western World. Partly it is that the problems of the Third World are so huge and so pressing that the temptation to go for grandiose but inadequately researched prophetic denunciation is irresistible. It is also partly due to the failure to produce a convincing social ethic for a pluralist world. JPIC might have provided a basis for this, but is still little more than a slogan. There is a lot more thinking to be done.

My ecumenical work in Britain during this period has centred mainly on the transition from the old British Council of Churches to the new ecumenical bodies with their much more comprehensive membership and their commitment to working through the churches, rather than on behalf of them. In September 1984 at the instigation of Philip Morgan, the then General Secretary of the BCC, I personally invited representatives of all the churches in Britain to a consultation, out of which grew the Inter-Church Meeting – which I then chaired. It was this meeting which in 1990 led to the setting up of the new bodies. The story of this development has been told elsewhere, and I will not repeat it. My own role, I think, was made possible by a combination of archiepiscopal status and long ecumenical involvement. The fact that I had time to devote to it illustrates one of the peculiar advantages of being at York.

Politics is not one of my main interests. Nevertheless an archbishop who tries to take the secular world seriously can hardly avoid it, particularly during a period of great social change and weak parliamentary opposition. The Church of England has been much criticized for its role during the Thatcher years, both by those who said it became too political, and by those who saw it as less than politically astute. The publication of *Faith in the City* in December 1985 restored some credit, but the truth is that at first few Christian spokesmen grasped the real nature of the change in Conservative political philosophy which had taken place. Indeed it was only when I started reading Hayek that I began to see the connection between some of the basic ideas of the New Right and Social Darwinism.

Mrs Thatcher had, at her own request, attended my enthronement, and in conversation afterwards had given my sermon 'eleven marks out of ten'.[5] This was a somewhat curious assessment because the sermon was about the erosion of public faith, and carried the strong implication that public policy and personal religion were to be seen as mutually influencing one another. In many subsequent exchanges with her Government this was one of the crucial points. Conservative philosophy needs to be able to appeal to a strong personal morality, both as a basis for the mutual trust on which a market economy depends, and also to offset such an economy's less desirable side-effects. What Conservative politicians have been less ready to acknowledge is that personal morality itself needs support from its social environment, and is therefore to some extent dependent on the character of the society which politicians help to create.

Exchanges about this mutual influence were largely sterile confrontations. The politicians tended to interpret any criticism of individualism as a relapse into collectivism, whereas the churches were generally trying to point out the significance of the erosion of community life. The churches in their turn were tempted to moralise about the evils of competition, and thus gave the impression of being content with inefficiency and waste.

The General Synod debate on the community charge, frequently cited as an example of gross political interference, can illustrate how minds were failing to meet one another. For some reason which was never wholly clear to me I was asked to lead the debate. It is not my kind of issue. I was therefore softer towards the Government than I might have been, and tried to put forward positive reasons why the charge might be justified. My criticisms were concentrated on the regressive nature of the taxation in that, apart from certain exceptions, the tax paid bore no relation to income. This seemed to me a moral, not a political point. What was not apparent at the time, however, was that the very idea of progressive principles of taxation had been consciously rejected. The Government instead seemed to be concerned only with accountability, while entertaining the false hope that voters would ascribe tax levels directly to local authorities. Synod and Government were speaking different languages.

The Gulf War presented a very different kind of challenge. Christian opinion was deeply divided. The bishops were criticized for not giving a clear lead, and there was much inconclusive discussion about whether or not the conditions for a Just War had been satisfied. Robert Runcie and I supported, with reservations, the need for military action.

In retrospect it seems to me that this hesitancy within the churches was both healthy and justified. It reflected the real complexity of the choices which had to be made, said enough to lend support to those who actually had to do the fighting, yet warned against too much self-congratulation or moral self-righteousness. It seized onto the hope, which seemed brighter then than it does now, that the United Nations could at last become an effective peacemaker. In preaching at the thanksgiving service after the war, I tried to express these conflicting emotions.[6]

Before the outset of hostilities I was also involved in a curious little adventure which may be a modest answer to the charge that in situations like this Christians should do more than talk. A Quaker friend with long diplomatic experience persuaded me that it was worth going to Iraq, on a strictly religious ticket, to try to appeal for a conciliatory response to the UN ultimatum on the basis of Islamic principles. He and I and an Islamic expert would travel there, and plans were laid with the help of an intermediary in Jordan. It was not until I was at Heathrow waiting for the others that a message came through from Jordan that our contacts there could not deliver their side of the arrangements, and we were advised not to travel. The air attacks began a few days later.

A further initiative before the war began led a year later to the publication of an impressive and well-documented Christian report on the arms trade, entitled *Profit without Honour?*[7] My own part in this was simply to persuade the Council on Christian Approaches to Defence and Disarmament, of which I am British President, to commission and sponsor the report, and the Archbishop of Canterbury to pay for it. The impetus given by the Gulf War to controlling arms sales now unfortunately seems to have been dissipated. Recent revelations about how the trade is actually conducted may help to get things moving again.

Media matters inevitably occupy much of an archbishop's time. I enjoy writing for newspapers, and find it a challenge to convey and commend Christian insights without making people of other persuasions switch off. There are those who feel they can only be truly Christian by constantly referring to Jesus and by bespattering their articles with texts. That may be fine for certain readerships. My own belief, however, is that for the people with whom I want to communicate it is the surest way of not being read.

I am less happy with radio and television. I am conscious that I do not perform well under the aggressive questioning which is nowadays supposed to make for good broadcasting. Generally I prefer to think before speaking. Moreover I am depressed by the narrowness and predictability of most of the questions which interviewers ask. I strongly suspect that there is a little file somewhere labelled 'Archbishop of York', and every time a researcher opens it, out pops the Bishop of Durham, or the notorious Crockford Preface, or the fact that as an adolescent I went through a phase of atheism. True, no doubt, but tedious. So let me at least try to dispose of the first two in the hope of closing the file.

Contrary to popular belief I had no hand in the appointment of David Jenkins as my successor at Durham. On the principle that one should not be involved in appointing one's own successor, I had arranged for another bishop to take my place on the Crown Appointments Commission. It did fall to me, however, to decide whether or not his consecration should proceed, given the controversy over his remarks in a television interview about the Virgin Birth and the bodily Resurrection of Jesus. I received a delegation, a petition, loads of letters with well-meaning but contradictory advice, and requests that his consecration should be postponed in order to allow the General Synod to debate the matter. In responding to requests for a postponement I set out my reasons for refusing it in a letter. I discussed the line I was proposing to take at a meeting of senior bishops, and received their approval. Among those present was the then Bishop of London, Graham Leonard.

It seemed to me that the main issue in the controversy was whether the Church of England was willing to take theological scholarship seriously. This willingness by no means implies the abandonment of basic Christian truths, but it should entail an open and uncensorious approach to the continuous process of testing and reinterpreting such truths. To set in motion what would in practice have amounted to a public heresy trial would have been to open the door to endless possible repressive action in the future. To allow the General Synod to decide, even in principle, whether a bishop should be consecrated would have been to exacerbate the dangerous tendency to make theological truth a matter of synodical decision. To postpone a consecration on the basis of public reaction to a television programme without taking into account an author's published work, seemed to me to be frivolous.

In fact David Jenkins had said nothing which would have surprised or shocked his fellow theologians. He had neither denied the Incarnation nor the Resurrection. In raising questions about the stories in which these fundamental doctrines are expressed, he had done no more than every theological student is required to do, and has constantly been done through Christian history. It has to be admitted that David Jenkins has a colourful way of expressing himself, and does not always make his meaning luminously clear. But the real problem underlying the subsequent furore was and is the gulf between theologians and the ordinary life of the church. A mixture of simple faith and unexplored doubt has kept many church members in ignorance of the cut-and-thrust of normal theological debate, and the media have been quick to exploit the fear and distrust latent in this separation. Furthermore the tide was running strongly in the direction of over-confident and dogmatic conservatism.

I was myself satisfied that David Jenkins could declare with

complete sincerity what the consecration service required him
to declare. If I had postponed his consecration in face of the
clamour I would have felt that I had betrayed an important
part of our Church of England heritage. The fact that some
people claimed the fire at York Minster as evidence that this
decision was mistaken, confirmed my belief that the main
issue was one of intellectual integrity.

The affair of the Crockford Preface was in some ways even
more bizarre, though with a much more tragic outcome. It,
too, was to a very large extent media-led, with the result that
the substantial and important issues Gareth Bennett had
raised in the first part of the Preface were almost wholly
sidetracked by the emphasis on personalities. I have fully
explained my own role in it elsewhere, and return to it now
only for some subsequent reflections and to correct a
persistent misinterpretation.[8]

At the time I made some strong criticisms of the, then
unknown, author. These have been interpreted as a dismissal
of the whole Preface, which was by no means the case. My
main and sharpest criticism was focused explicitly on serious
accusations against both archbishops about the conduct of the
Crown Appointments Commission. These were damaging,
untrue and could only have been based on hearsay. In my view
they took the Preface well beyond its traditional role of
providing sharp-eyed criticism of the Church, towards something much more dangerously destructive. The author's
suicide, like all suicides, enormously enhanced guilt feelings
on all sides, and I believe its repercussions did immeasurable
harm to the Church of England.

In retrospect it all seems so unnecessary. Gareth Bennett
was perceptive, scholarly and articulate. He was a well-
respected figure in the General Synod, having been elected to
its Standing Committee. Between the writing of his Preface
and its publication he had sat on one occasion as a member of
the Crown Appointments Commission, and must have begun
to see how false his account of it was. He was the intellectual
mentor of the Anglo-Catholic wing of the Church, and could
have had the opportunity to engage in constructive thinking
about how it might emerge from its rather introverted and
negative stance. But he was also, unfortunately, a somewhat
lonely and frustrated don, not without a taste for intrigue,

who felt that his gifts had not been fully used by the Church, and who had a greater gift for historical analysis than for leadership. He was adept at picking to pieces an argument. But many found it hard to imagine him as a bishop. Had he been able to withstand the exposure of his authorship, weather the temporary storm, restate his criticisms in more forward-looking terms, and accept that his colleagues actually valued his contribution, the recent history of the Church of England might have been different.

As I write this, five and a half years later, media attention towards the Church of England is centred on the ordination of women to the priesthood. Recent months have seen innumerable headlines predicting the demise of the Church of England, and it is not surprising that there are many worried people who are fearful of what the future might hold. My own policy has been to try to look positively at the difficult choices which have to be made in order to maintain the diverse character of the Church, and to see in this delicately balanced process of living together a gift and witness the Church can offer to a divided world.

It is fundamental to my theology that God is concerned with the whole world, today a world full of murderous oppositions, attempting to come to terms with pluralism, and constantly flying off into a polarization between fanaticisms. The Church, as a sign of the Kingdom of God, has to live within this maelstrom, and can either be sucked into it by itself becoming polarized into irreconcilable opposites; or it can find ways of respecting differences, living with them, and celebrating those things which unite us. The Church of England has managed to live with such diversity hitherto. In so far as any church does so, it can be for the healing of the nations. I believe this can still be our role, not because we are better or wiser than other traditions, for manifestly that would not be true. Nor can we claim to have avoided fudging issues in the past, smoothing over differences or ignoring difficulties. But the way we characteristically do things as a Church can, or should, speak loudly of the sheer givenness of the grace of God. Infant baptism, sacramentality, our parochial structure, our openness to all, our deep historical roots in the life of the nation, all in their different ways are expressions of the givenness of grace.

And it is by acknowledging that grace, and graciously accepting one another, that we shall be a healed and healing church in the days ahead. That is where I see my own agenda.

Notes

1. M. Duggan, *Runcie* (Hodder and Stoughton 1983), p. 174.
2. e.g. Colossians 3.18—4.1. The principle of borrowing from contemporary moral codes is taken much further in the Pastoral Epistles.
3. see above, Chapter 7.
4. The story is told in D. Gosling, *A New Earth*. CCBI 1992.
5. Published in *Confessions of a Conservative Liberal* (SPCK 1988), pp. 7–9.
6. see above, Interlude: The Gulf War.
7. Obtainable from CCADD, St Bride Foundation Institute, Bride Lane, London EC3Y 8EQ.
8. *Confessions of a Conservative Liberal*, pp. 82–91.